The publisher and the University of California Press Foundation gratefully acknowledge the generous support of the George Gund Foundation Imprint in African American Studies.

Ella Baker's Catalytic Leadership

COMMUNICATION FOR SOCIAL JUSTICE ACTIVISM

Series Editors
Patricia S. Parker, *University of North Carolina at Chapel Hill*
Lawrence R. Frey, *University of Colorado Boulder*

Ella Baker's Catalytic Leadership

A PRIMER ON COMMUNITY ENGAGEMENT
AND COMMUNICATION FOR SOCIAL
JUSTICE

Patricia S. Parker

UNIVERSITY OF CALIFORNIA PRESS

University of California Press
Oakland, California

© 2020 by Patricia S. Parker

Library of Congress Cataloging-in-Publication Data

Names: Parker, Patricia Sue, 1958- author.
Title: Ella Baker's catalytic leadership : a primer on community
    engagement and communication for social justice / Patricia S. Parker.
Other titles: Communication for social justice activism ; 2.
Description: Oakland, California : University of California Press, [2020] |
    Series: Communication for social justice activism; 2 | Includes
    bibliographical references and index.
Identifiers: LCCN 2020014483 (print) | LCCN 2020014484 (ebook) |
    ISBN 9780520300903 (cloth) | ISBN 9780520300910 (paperback) |
    ISBN 9780520972094 (epub)
Subjects: LCSH: Ella Baker Women's Center for Leadership and
    Community Activism. | African American leadership—North
    Carolina—Chapel Hill—Case studies. | Community leadership—
    North Carolina—Chapel Hill—Case studies. | Social justice—North
    Carolina—Chapel Hill. | African American women—Social conditions.
Classification: LCC E185.615 .P3355 2020 (print) | LCC E185.615
    (ebook) | DDC 323.092 [B]—dc23
LC record available at https://lccn.loc.gov/2020014483
LC ebook record available at https://lccn.loc.gov/2020014484

29 28 27 26 25 24 23 22 21 20
10 9 8 7 6 5 4 3 2 1

In loving memory of my sister, Mayola

Contents

Illustrations

Preface

When I give talks about Ella Baker's social justice leadership at community gatherings or academic conferences, I often start by asking how many in the audience have heard of the Reverend Dr. Martin Luther King Jr. The audience will laugh nervously as everyone in the room raises their hands. Then I'll ask how many have heard of Ella Baker. In a room of, say, one hundred people, perhaps one or two hands will go up. More often, none do.

But by many historical accounts, Ella Baker was as influential as Dr. King in shaping the arc of the US Civil Rights Movement of the 1960s, which brought about sweeping changes that advanced social justice (see, e.g., Payne, 1995/2007); Ransby, 2003; Robnett, 1996). In the colloquial language of contemporary social movements, Ella Baker mobilized with the *grassroots* while Dr. King mobilized with the *grass tops*.[1]

Ella Baker and other Black women grassroots leaders, such as Septima Clark and Rosa Parks, epitomized catalyzing, community-based approaches to social justice activism during the Civil Rights Movement. These approaches contrast sharply with Dr. King's legacy as a vital motivator and mass movement builder (Jensen & Hammerback, 2000). Both of these facets of social justice leadership—grassroots community organizing for strategic action and macro mobilizing for large-scale action—were interrelated and necessary to advance the Civil Rights Movement (see Branch, 1988/2007; Holsaert et al., 2010; Robnett, 1996). However, Ella Baker's leadership, and that of many others, has been comparatively invisible in the scholarly and mainstream historical record (A. F. Scott, 1990).[2] Sociologist Belinda Robnett has coined the term "bridge leadership" to depict this vital behind-the-scenes work of the Civil Rights Movement, carried out mostly by Black women in the segregated communities of the Jim Crow South. She has described this leadership as a process of micro mobilization wherein Black women provided the "bridges necessary to cross boundaries between the personal lives of potential constituents and adherents and the political life of civil rights movement organizations" (1996, p. 1664). Much has been written about how Dr. King's rhetorical style mobilized grassroots action, as well as about the philosophies, such as nonviolent resistance, that he championed as foundational strategies for the US Civil Rights Movement (Branch, 1988/2007; Lucaites & Condit, 1990; Hohle, 2013). There has been far less attention to the on-the-ground bridge leadership developed in Baker's philosophy.

That situation is changing. By 2019, several new essays and books had been written about Ella Baker's influence in social movement history. Communication scholars in rhetoric and critical organizational communication have been among those leading the charge to excavate her hidden influence (DeLaure, 2008; Orthy, 2016; Parker, 2004). The internet has created pathways for more public awareness of Baker's legacy, as it has for other hidden histories. By now, for example, many people know that Rosa Parks was a seasoned activist long before her well-known act of resistance during the 1955 Montgomery, Alabama, bus boycott (McGuire, 2010, p. xvii). A recent Google search of Ella Baker's name yielded more than fifteen million results, providing some indication of her legacy and contemporary impact. The Ella Baker Center for Human Rights in Oakland, California, cofounded by CNN news commentator and program host Van Jones, is one of the more visible and well-known entities among dozens around the world that now bear her name (see Orthy, 2016).

Moreover, thousands of people consider themselves either direct descendants or second- or third-generation carriers of Baker's social justice leadership philosophy. Her tradition has been passed on through written and oral histories, endowed professorships and lectures, and activities of social change organizations and youth leadership programs (Holsaert et al., 2010; Orthy, 2016; Ransby, 2003). These homages to Ella Baker's legacy are not mere exercises of historical memory. Rather, they signal a commitment among contemporary social justice activists and scholars to the continuing relevance of her philosophy, especially her group-centered approaches to engaging knowledge that is often marginalized or excluded, especially in the elite spaces of the academy.

This book builds on the new visibility of Baker's work and pushes back against the persistent invisibility and erasure that still characterize Black women's and girls' leadership and activism. In mainstream scholarly literature on community organizing and social movements, and also in public discourse, including online platforms such as Twitter, Facebook, and Instagram, Black women are still invisible, erased, and subjected both to forms of violence and to a persistent unwillingness to acknowledge this violence. For example, three Black women—Alicia Garza, Patrisse Cullors, and Opal Tometi—created #BlackLivesMatter as a response to anti-Black racism and as "a call to action for Black people after 17-year-old Trayvon Martin was posthumously placed on trial for his own murder and the killer, George Zimmerman, was not held accountable for the crime he committed" (Garza, 2014). At this writing, it is a global movement that has successfully popularized radical discourse and vibrantly modeled democratic participation through social media and street-based activism (Ransby, 2018; Rickford, 2016). It is also an example of how Black women leaders, including two queer activists, are quickly and momentously erased once movements gain popular momentum. As Garza explains: "Straight men, unintentionally or intentionally, have taken the work of queer Black women and erased our contributions. Perhaps if we were the charismatic Black men many are rallying around [the Black Lives Matter Movement] these days, it would have been a different story, but being Black queer women in this society (and apparently within these movements) tends to equal invisibility and non-relevancy" (Garza, 2014).

Garza, Cullors, and Tometi's experiences are linked to those of bridge leaders such as Ella Baker and Rosa Parks who came before them; both sets of activists have contended with the persistent intersection of sexism and White supremacy in Western culture (Banet-Weiser & Miltner, 2016; Daniels, 2009; Lawson, 2018). Bailey and Trudy (2018) coined the term *misogynoir* in 2008 to describe the particular form of racialized sexism that Black women experience, especially in online media platforms but also in everyday life. On the one hand, social spaces online and offline render Black women invisible and silence their voices, not only in social justice movements but also in boardrooms and the halls of academia (Bell & Nkomo, 2001; Collins, 1989; Parker, 2001; Sesko & Biernat, 2010). On the other hand, Black women become hypervisible and vulnerable to attack precisely because of their Blackness. The online harassment of *Saturday Night Live* comedienne Leslie Jones is one example of vicious attacks against Black women in online platforms (see Lawson, 2018). In 2016, Jones had a starring role in the remake of the 1984 blockbuster film *Ghostbusters*, which had an all-female cast in the parts played by top male actors in the original film. What began as a backlash against the remake quickly transformed into a sustained misogynist and racist attack on Leslie Jones's character and physical appearance (Howard, 2016). Left unchecked, these kinds of attacks not only reify misogynist and racialized tropes but also help to legitimize intrapersonal, interpersonal, systemic, and state-supported violence against Black girls and women (Crenshaw, 2013).[3]

As a counternarrative, this book joins the voices reclaiming and advancing Black women's and girls' voices, agency, and activism in the scholarly literature, in public discourse, and in grassroots organizing for social justice (Brown, 2013; Cruz, 2017; Gumbs, 2016; Love & Duncan, 2017; Parker, 2004). It describes a case study that centers the voices of African American teen girls and their allies who live in a segregated neighborhood of an affluent college town. The girls are part of a small collective of students, parents, university faculty, and community activists who are learning leadership in the spirit of Ella Baker.

For too long, what Black women have learned through centuries of antiracist and antisexist organizing has been co-opted, taken for granted, or ignored (hooks, 1989; Rebecca A., 2018; A. F. Scott, 1990). That tradition of social justice leadership can and should be engaged in the current moment of political ferment. Ella Baker's praxis—the connection of theory to practice—can lead the way.

CODA

As this book is in production in June 2020, the world is actively engaging and fighting two pandemics: COVID-19, a deadly coronavirus that has created a global health and economic crisis on a massive scale; and the persistent scourge of racism and anti-Black violence. In March 2020, as the world began to shelter in place to slow the spread of the coronavirus, COVID-19 laid bare the disproportionate impacts on vulnerable communities due to inequities in access to economic, education, and health care among Blacks, Latinx, Native peoples, and other marginalized groups in the United States. Then, on May 25, a viral video circulated that showed a White police officer in Minneapolis, Minnesota, kneeling on the neck of George Floyd, an unarmed Black man, lying handcuffed on the pavement, for eight minutes and forty-six seconds, as Mr. Floyd repeated the phrase, "I can't breathe" and three other police officers looked on. Mr. Floyd's killing by the police was just one of the myriad acts of police/state-supported brutality and vigilante violence against Black people—including Breonna Taylor, Ahmaud Arbery, Michael Brown Jr., Trayvon Martin, and countless others—that have been repeated throughout our four-hundred-year history in the United States.

The outrage over George Floyd's murder has sparked protests in cities and rural areas across the United States and around the world. People from all backgrounds are marching in support of the Black Lives Matter movement and calls for the kind of social justice leadership and transformative change modeled in Ella Baker's praxis. Change is happening. On June 7, the Minneapolis City Council announced a plan to disband the police department and invest in proven community-led public safety approaches in Minneapolis. I see the spirit of Ella Baker in the work of community-based activists like Kandace Montgomery, part of the lead team in Black Lives Matters Minneapolis; the leaders of the Black Youth Project of Durham, North Carolina; and others from around the United States and globally who have been laboring in their communities to dismantle structural racism and work toward a true democracy, as Ms. Baker envisioned. This book is meant to honor that work and catalyze other work like it.

Acknowledgments

I am deeply grateful to the many people whose support helped bring this book to fruition. It brings me great joy to acknowledge them here. Lyn Uhl, my editor at the University of California Press, expertly guided the multilayered processes that birthed this book and the series in which it appears. Thank you, Lyn, for championing the "Ella Baker book" and sharing your editorial genius to bring it to life. To Larry Frey, my coeditor for the Communication and Social Justice Activism series, thank you for your leadership in helping to advance this important area of our field. I also owe a debt of gratitude to Enrique Ochoa-Kaup, Niels Hooper, and Kim Robinson at the Press, and to the peer reviewers who provided detailed and productive feedback to strengthen the final manuscript.

Along the way, I was fortunate to have several colleagues serve as informal readers, writing partners, and interlocutors, including Arthur Romano, Sarah Dempsey, Dottie Holland, Larry Grossberg, and members of my writers' group at the UNC Institute for the Arts and Humanities. Faith Holsaert, who as a young activist knew and worked with Ella Baker, read early drafts of my proposal and helped boost my confidence as a writer. Marlo Goldstein Hode read every page of the draft manuscript, providing insightful feedback that helped me see my own thinking more clearly. I am immensely appreciative of their support.

Community-engaged scholarship and teaching, like the work represented in this volume, is accomplished through the generous support of both institutional and external funding. I gratefully acknowledge support from the following at UNC–Chapel Hill: Cobey First Year Seminars Course Development Fund, Carolina Center for Public Service, APPLES Service-Learning, Kenan-Biddle Partnership, Robertson Foundation, Institute for the Arts and Humanities, and the Department of Communication. This work also benefited from resources provided by the Strowd Roses Foundation and Elayne Dorsey at the W.K. Kellogg Foundation.

This work stands as a testament to the power of collectives working toward social justice. I am grateful for the opportunity to work alongside the girls and their families represented in this book, the students from the COMM 089/053 first-year seminars, and the many volunteers and community partners that supported the work over the years. A special thanks to the board members of the Ella Baker Women's Center for their continued guidance and support.

Finally, I want to acknowledge the support of my remarkable family, who are a constant source of kindness, joy, and unconditional love. I'm grateful to have my local North Carolina crew: my son, Patrick; his lovely partner, Morgan; and my sister, Willette. My other siblings are only a text message away: Eric, Richard, Jurlene, Zora, Helen, Carolyn, Alvin, George, Debra, and Mary. Thank you for keeping Mother and Daddy's legacy of love going strong. We miss our big sister, Mayola, whose passing last year still seems surreal. This book is dedicated to her memory.

Introduction

I believe that the struggle is eternal. Somebody else carries on.

Ella Baker (1980)

I think, as a young girl, I've seen a lot of stuff, and been
through a lot of stuff at my age. . . . I think it's a personal
thing when a person goes through something and, you
know, so many people take that stress to like killing themselves. . . . I want to start a group at my school at lunchtime,
with a whole bunch of girls—'cause I'm just working with
girls—where they sit around and talk about it . . . we could
just talk about our feelings and what's going on with our
life and how we should deal with it.

Jamilla, age fourteen (March 10, 2010)[1]

Ella Josephine Baker (1903–1986) was a civil rights and human rights
activist whose career as a behind-the-scenes organizer spanned more than
fifty years. Her legacy continues to inspire social justice activists around
the world to be someone—like Jamilla, quoted above—who "carries on" the
struggle for freedom, perhaps infusing it with new meanings given the context of the time. For Baker, inspiration came from her childhood experiences growing up in a tight-knit Black community, only one generation
away from the end of institutionalized slavery in the United States. She
was born in Norfolk, Virginia, but raised from age seven in rural Littleton,
North Carolina, near the area where both sets of her grandparents had
been enslaved.[2] She grew up hearing their stories of struggle and suffering,
as well as how they fought back and resisted whenever possible to preserve
their dignity. She also heard stories of their belief in self-determination and

support for the betterment of the community. For example, by 1888 her maternal grandparents, Mitchell and Josephine Elizabeth (Bet) Ross, along with Mitchell's brothers and cousins, had worked for decades to save enough money to buy land from the estate that had previously enslaved them. They immediately donated a portion of the land for the construction of a local church, where Mitchell Ross served as a well-respected member of the clergy and which also housed a school for African Americans. The Rosses had become landowners when most Black families in the rural South, like Baker's paternal grandparents, Teema and Margaret Baker, were trapped in a tenant farming system that for many didn't seem that different from slavery.

The historian Barbara Ransby has observed that the class distinctions in Ella Baker's family helped shape her consciousness about class. Baker came to believe, as her grandparents and parents had taught, that those in a position to help others had a duty to do so. But she also believed that those in elite positions should "humble themselves in order to create the social space necessary for the more oppressed people in the community to speak and act on their own behalf" (Ransby, 2003, pp. 44–45). Over time, Baker continued to hone this thinking into a radical vision for participative democracy as she allied herself with poor and oppressed people working to change unjust systems.

Gender roles were also challenged in Baker's community, providing a foundation for her to confront the sexist norms she later encountered in male-dominated early and mid-twentieth-century change organizations. Ella Baker's parents, Blake Baker, a maritime worker, and Georgianna (Anna) Ross Baker, a teacher, had moved to Norfolk soon after their marriage in 1896 to seek economic opportunity in the city, as did an increasing number of African Americans living in the rural South at the time. It was a period of increasing White terror that often followed Black prosperity in the United States in the Jim Crow era. By 1910, as the family had grown to include three children—Blake Curtis, Ella, and Maggie—Anna Ross Baker returned to Littleton for the security of the strong community ties there. Blake Baker kept his job in Norfolk and visited the family on weekends and holidays. Mitchell Ross, who had recognized his granddaughter's gifts as a thinker (even at age six), had passed away the previous year.

Ella Baker's mother and maternal grandmother thus became the strongest influences in her life, instilling in her a sense of confidence that women could, and indeed had a duty to, work for the betterment of their communities. Anna Ross Baker, in particular, was a strong role model for her daughters. She worked as an activist in local church groups to help advocate for education and to promote antilynching campaigns. She became one of the leaders in the National Black Baptist Convention movement that carved out a space for women's activism in the male-dominated Black church. Ella Baker would do the same in later decades but on a much broader scale.

At age fourteen, Ella Baker left home to attend Shaw University in Raleigh, North Carolina, which at the time was both a boarding school and a college.[3] While at Shaw, Baker began to establish her identity as an activist and began her lifelong work as an intellectual and political organizer. Reflecting on that time when she was not yet the rebel she later became, Baker remarked, "I didn't break rules, but I challenged rules" (1977, p. 30). In addition to her budding activism, Baker was growing intellectually and honing her political ideology toward coalition building across lines of race, gender, and geographies. She read the works of Kant, Socrates, Aristotle, and Carter G. Woodson and studied the lives of Frederick Douglass, Harriet Tubman, and Sojourner Truth.[4] Already an impressive communicator, at Shaw, Baker further honed her communication capacities as a member of the debate team and through her service as associate editor for the *Shaw University Journal*. Baker was an exceptional student. She graduated valedictorian of her class from both high school in 1923 and college in 1927.[5] Defying her mother's expectation that she would become a teacher, Baker headed to New York City. There, she continued to hone her leadership philosophy, which envisioned an approach to participative democracy inclusive of people living under the heels of oppression.

Baker also broadened her influence through her philosophical debates with leftist intellectuals and critical thinkers, especially during the years of political ferment and organizing from the 1930s through the 1960s (James, 1994; Ransby, 2003). She also carved out a space for her leadership in the predominantly male political circles that included W. E. B. Du Bois, Thurgood Marshall, and the Reverend Dr. Martin Luther King Jr. Across the span of her career, "she was involved in more than thirty major political campaigns and organizations, addressing such issues as the war in Vietnam, Puerto Rican independence, South African apartheid, politi-cal repression, prison conditions, poverty, unequal education, and sexism" (Ransby, 2003, pp. 5–6).

Above all, Ella Baker was a conduit through which the legacy of Black resistance and transformative change processes was passed from her genera-tion to future ones. This is perhaps one of the most enduring aspects of Baker's contributions to social justice philosophy. As exemplified in the words that introduced this chapter, Baker believed that the protracted strug-gle for freedom was carried on by those who brought the struggle forward within the context of the times. This was most evident in her work with youth at the forefront of the 1960s era Civil Rights Movement.[6] It was Ella Baker's influence that ensured the creation of the autonomous Student Nonviolent Coordinating Committee (SNCC) (Payne, 1995/2007, pp. 95–96). However, as Ransby has explained in her sweeping and well-documented biography of Ella Baker's life, Baker's concern was not simply about the autonomy of the young activists of SNCC (pronounced "snick"). Rather, she saw in the youth leading the sit-ins of the 1960s "the brazen fighting spirit the students had exhibited in their sit-in-protests ... [and] ... enormous promise in their courageous actions, their creativity, and their openness to new forms of struggle, and she wanted to give them the space and freedom for that poten-tial to develop" (Ransby, 2003, p. 244). She mentored the young leaders of SNCC and others who joined the movement, freely sharing the ideas she had honed over a lifetime of social justice activism.

. . . .

This book tells the story of some of the early twenty-first-century conduits of Ella Baker's philosophy. It is about people in vulnerable communities working in partnership with people in well-resourced organizations to develop their capacities to lead social justice action. In the case of African American girls like Jamilla, quoted at the begin-ning of this chapter, and other girls of color who live in underresourced, segregated, subsidized housing, this book is about the potential for their coming to consciousness about social activism. Their activism often happens within the context of strict housing policies that threaten basic security and other street-level systems of control that constitute a "new Jim Crow" era in the United States, and whose tactics reach into neighborhoods and schools.[7] It happens in the context of mass incarceration and anti-immigrant tactics. Globally, inclusive of the United States, girls and women face persistent threats of violence as they expose and challenge misogynistic cultures.

This book is also about the limits and possibilities of alliances with people like me—an African American woman with a PhD, a university researcher and tenured professor at an elite Research I state university, a feminist, and an activist—who come from outside of the community to support social justice leadership. People from outside communities— such as scholar-activists, university student–service learners, and policy professionals—are not immune to exercises of power; even the most progressive scholar-activists may (unwittingly or not) become instruments of state or corporate power, reinforcing some of the very injustices they aspire to work against (Brown, 2015). Indeed, current trends in engagement between organizations and communities for social change have tended to advance a neoliberal project, in the sense that community voices are systematically erased by ostensibly participatory interventions that are actually instruments to further the search for new markets and new sources of raw materials (Dutta, 2011). Neoliberal projects often contribute to the development of "Oppression Olympics," in which different groups are pitted against one another to fight for scarce resources (Yuval-Davis, 2012).

Strengthening communication capacities for coalition building and solidarity in social justice activism requires that multiple and intersecting kinds of power be made legible through a "decolonizing" approach that gets to the root causes of problems. Without that kind of legibility, we can miss clues about neoliberal processes that erase or distort community voices. A decolonizing approach to research and policy checks how power is operating in collaborations between organizations and communities to level the field of possibilities (Chakrabarty, 2002; Dutta, 2015). Ella Baker's praxis calls for that kind of legibility, as I learned through my attempts to perform university-community engagement with girls and their families in vulnerable communities.

.   .   .   .   .

In the summer of 2005, I was volunteering at the Family Resource Center at Regal Gardens and University Heights, two predominantly African American public housing complexes not far from UNC–Chapel Hill, where I am a faculty member.[8] It is not unusual for even longtime residents to express surprise that there are "low-income housing projects" in College Town. Regal Gardens and University Heights are situated in the historically African American part of College Town, two blocks from the fashionable Main Street that forms the center of the city.[9] The housing complexes were built on a sloping hill, separated from each other by a busy street that slices through the neighborhood en route to the many affluent neighborhoods in the city. University Heights sits at the top of the slope and has fifteen newer duplex units and a large courtyard and playground in the center. Regal Gardens is much older, constructed in the early 1950s, and has four buildings of ten two- and three-bedroom apartments that continue down toward the bottom of the slope and abut a thick wooded area. People who are experiencing homelessness sometimes spend the night in the wooded area behind Regal Gardens. A path that leads from the park at the edge of the wooded area to a small playground at Regal Gardens is often used as a shortcut to get into the center of town. For cars, there is only one way in and out of each of the complexes, and police responding to residents' calls for assistance regularly lock down the entrances.

I contemplated the prospects of becoming a more community-engaged scholar-activist and my position as a Black woman academic. I was very aware of the crisis conditions facing Black women because of structural inequality in the United States: high rates of unemployment, increasing rates of incarceration, disenfranchisement, and health-care disparity (see Pratt-Clarke, 2013). These conditions especially captured the vulnerability of Black girls and women living in the growing number of segregated spaces created by the "new Jim Crow" context. And there was evidence that government officials and policy makers were not paying attention to the crisis. For example, as Cohen (2004) reported, when journalist Gwen Ifill moderated the 2004 vice presidential debate between then Vice President Dick Cheney and vice presidential candidate John Edwards, she alerted the nation to the HIV/AIDS health crisis facing African American women, which was apparently news to the candidates.[10] "I want to talk to you about AIDS," she said. "And not about AIDS in China or Africa, but AIDS right here in this country where Black women between the ages of 25 and 44 are 13 times more likely to die of the disease. What should the government's role be in helping to end the growth of this epidemic?" Vice President Cheney did not deny his ignorance. "I have not heard those numbers with respect to African-American women. I was not aware that it was—that they're in epidemic there," he said. John Edwards decided to evade the question, focusing instead on AIDS in Africa, the genocide in Sudan, uninsured Americans, and presidential hopeful John Kerry. Despite US policy makers' lag in taking up the charge to protect Black women and girls, at conferences and in community conversations I was connecting with women who *were* acting to engage Black girls and women. They included women who lived in towns not far from UNC–Chapel Hill and nearby Duke University and were creating their own survival in their own neighborhoods.

In retrospect, what I was witnessing in the early 2000s was a resurgence of the late nineteenth-century Black women's club movement that Ella Baker's mother, Anna Ross Baker, had been a part of. This was a movement of thousands of women-led church groups, social clubs, sororities, and other organizations in Black civil society that responded to the intense racial hatred, violence, and segregation African Americans faced in the Jim Crow era, the period just after the end of the institutionalized enslavement of African Americans. These organizations were at the height of their activity in the mid-twentieth century. They provided not only a safe haven but also "a set of institutions, communication networks, and practices that facilitated responses to economic and political challenges confronting Black people" (Collins, 1998, p. 23; see also Dawson, 1995).

Black women–led organizing was on the rise again in the early 2000s. Kimberly Springer's *Still Lifting, Still Climbing: African American Women's Contemporary Activism* described the legacy of leadership and activism in Black women's history and noted the "historical continuity" of activism led by African American women (1999, p. 2). Springer chose as her starting point the legacy of the National Association of Colored Women (NACW), which in 1895 merged two national organizations of Black women's clubs. The NACW motto was "lifting as we climb," emphasizing the organization's commitment to community and its roots in a culture of resistance that began in the era of US institutionalized slavery. Springer's book surveyed the growing numbers of Black women–led organizations and their various causes that were alive and well in 1999. Her book described new kinds of oppression in Black communities at the dawn of the twenty-first century, but also the ways that Black women were once again responding to them. I felt a calling to join in this intervention.

FOUNDING THE ELLA BAKER WOMEN'S CENTER FOR LEADERSHIP AND COMMUNITY ACTIVISM

Tenured in 2004, I felt I had the academic freedom to expand the boundaries of my research into a program of community-engaged scholarship.[11] Significantly, UNC–Chapel Hill was among the campuses nationwide that were building the infrastructure of support for engaged scholarship, such as engagement-focused research grants and research and study leaves. In 2006, I received two competitive awards through the UNC–Chapel Hill College of Arts and Sciences: the Kauffman Foundation's Faculty Fellowship for Social Entrepreneurship and a competitive research leave at the Institute for the Arts and Humanities. Those awards provided crucial resources. They afforded me the time away from teaching and service for more in-depth study of Ella Baker's organizing praxis and opportunities to engage with Black women organizers in communities locally and across the country who seemed to be organizing in the spirit of Ella Baker. They also provided access to a paid consultant, who helped me establish the Ella Baker Women's Center for Leadership and Community Activism as a nonprofit and community-based organization in 2007.[12] The center would support a newly formed collaboration with African American girls (ages thirteen to seventeen) and their adult allies in the two previously mentioned neighborhoods near the university.

To further prepare for the launch of the center, I networked at conferences and community gatherings (social media had not yet become the primary means for networking, at least not for me) to learn from Black women community-based leaders. Four in particular were crucial to the emergence of the Ella Baker Women's Center. Cynthia Brown was a local community organizer whose antiracism work on economic and environmental justice grounded her in urban and rural communities across the state. She taught workshops that became central to our critical pedagogy. She had formed an antiracist organization, Dismantling Racism, that was in high demand across the country. Nia Wilson, executive director of Spirit House in Durham, North Carolina, became an important ally in our work against the prison-industrial complex. Two other key allies were Delores Bailey, executive director at EmPOWERment, Inc., a community-based organization that works with families to achieve homeownership, and Ms. Vergie, a resident and activist in the Regal Gardens and University Heights neighborhoods.[13] These two community experts worked most closely with my students and me as we launched and developed the Ella Baker Women's Center's work for social justice leadership.

.   .   .   .   .

Since its founding in 2007, the Ella Baker Women's Center has provided a training ground for undergraduate student–service learners and graduate student researchers interested in learning a critical engagement praxis that centers community knowledge. Service learning is an experiential educa-tion methodology based on reciprocal learning, wherein both providers and recipients of service benefit from the activities (Furco 1996; Sigman, 1979). In 2009, I designed a course that applied such an approach, a first-year seminar called Models of Collective Leadership for Social Change (COMM 89/53). The course was designed for transfer students and stu-dents in their first or second semester of university study, who could spend their remaining college years applying the capacities they learned in the course. The seminar allows students to explore the critical questions, dis-cussed later, related to community-based partnerships. During the first five weeks of the seminar, students critically reflect on ideas from readings, guest speakers, documentary films, and case studies to explore questions relevant to "power elites" (e.g., university stakeholders, nongovernmental/ nonprofit organizations) who work alongside people in vulnerable com-munities to create positive social change. The course also equips students with applied knowledge about a vast array of communication pedagogies and participatory praxis, such as photovoice, oral histories, community dialogues, and arts activism. (The Ella Baker Women's Center employed these tools, and they are discussed in subsequent chapters.) Students then applied that knowledge in diverse teams formed in partnership with community-based organizations or community members who had identified a need and desire to collaborate with service-learning students to complete projects. From 2009 to 2013, the center served as one of four service-learning organizations partnering with our class. At the center, student teams worked with African American teen girls to plan and implement several projects, including the Sharing the Mantle Conference, which showcased their collaborative work and best practices in campus/community partnerships for social justice. Many of the COMM 89/53 students stayed connected with their partnering organizations (including the Ella Baker Women's Center). Students who have stayed in touch tell me that they have gone on to start social justice organizations of their own or are applying what they've learned in public and private sector work around the world.

Graduate student researchers have also advanced the work of the center while honing their own capacities as community-based researchers. These students worked with me to develop and present critical pedagogy workshops and conduct research (Mease & Terry, 2012).

Finally, the Moore Undergraduate Research Apprenticeship Program (MURAP) at the University of North Carolina at Chapel Hill is another student research and learning experience that was critical in advancing the work of the center. Founded in 1993, this program attracts students from colleges and universities throughout the United States to spend ten weeks in the summer preparing to apply to graduate school. I served as a research mentor from 1999 through 2010 and worked with eight students who spent their summers helping to build the work of the Ella Baker Women's Center. It was the critical work of two MURAP students, Joaquín Sánchez and Elisa Oceguera, that laid the groundwork for the center's flagship program, Striving Sisters Speak!, to emerge and thrive.

Striving Sisters Speak! (S3!) is the girl-centered leadership group that was founded and named in 2007 by the initial cohort of seven teen girls from University Heights and Regal Gardens in College Town. With these girls at the center, a collective of graduate student volunteers, undergraduate summer research interns, and community activists organized to support the emerging participatory research project. S3! leadership cohorts have become a flagship program to create and implement social justice leadership projects at the Ella Baker Women's Center (see Parker et al., 2011). Over the course of the six-year period reported in this book (2007–2013), S3! cohorts and university- and community-based allies have worked collaboratively to produce several youth-led social justice projects, including (a) researching root causes of state violence and structural inequality, which the girls presented at youth conferences they helped to organize; (b) organizing social justice campaigns, including efforts to "raise the age" limits to end youth incarceration in adult prisons; and (c) creating and presenting youth arts activist projects to advance antiracist civic education. These concrete examples and others from the center's work are described in subsequent chapters. They illustrate a communication framework and lessons learned for productive university-community collaborations in the paradoxical context in which they are situated.

.   .   .   .   .

Ella Baker had what I introduce in this book as a catalytic leadership approach, a decolonizing praxis that is applicable to organizational-community collaborations. *Catalytic leadership* is a concrete set of communication practices for doing social justice leadership in equitable partnership *with*, instead of *on*, communities. I first encountered Ella Baker's ideas while researching a book on African American women executives' leadership (Parker, 2004). The participants' oral histories were filled with references to legacies of leadership wisdom passed on to them that, I argued, represented a tradition of leadership in Black women's history of antiracist resistance. Ella Baker embodied that tradition. Since then, I have continued to study Baker through archival research and on-the-ground praxis. My understanding of Baker's approach to social justice leadership is heavily influenced by the work of historians Charles Payne (1989) and Barbara Ransby (2001, 2003). It was Payne who amplified Ella Baker's approach as "group centered" as opposed to "leader centered." In other words, Baker believed that people in communities could learn to lead themselves on important issues, centering the decision-making power in the group working for social justice instead of having a charismatic leader decide what action to take. Ransby's account provided a nuanced interpretation of Baker's philosophy "based on militant antiracism, grassroots popular democracy, a subversion of traditional class and gender hierarchies, and a long-term vision for fundamental social and economic change" (2001, p. 43). To better understand Baker's group-centered approach and philosophy, I also analyzed her writing, speeches, and interviews archived at the Schomburg Center for Black Culture in Harlem, New York; the UNC–Chapel Hill Libraries; and the Veterans of the Civil Rights Movement archives at Duke University's Center for Documentary Studies.

Using those sources as a starting point for my understanding of Ella Baker's catalytic leadership, this book describes my own experience as the founding director of the Ella Baker Women's Center for Leadership and Community Activism. The center's mission is to advance the legacy and work of Ella Baker through contemporary interventions for social justice. The book covers the first six years of work after the center's founding in 2007. My account of this history oscillates between the stories of African American girls at the center, developing their capacities as leaders, and the university-based and community allies supporting them. Ultimately it foregrounds the dynamism of the partnership for social justice activism that made up the collective.

The case is an example of university-community partnerships, but readers will find it relevant to other organization types, such as large nongovernmental agencies, state agencies with strategic community initiatives, or other programmatic initiatives that engage with people in vulnerable communities. More important, anyone in pursuit of social justice will find Ella Baker's philosophy of praxis to be relevant.

EIGHT QUESTIONS

Questions Ella Baker was asking in the 1930s through the 1980s are still relevant in the 2000s. I offer the following eight questions, which undergird the case study, as helpful guides for your work. First: *Under what conditions do people living in vulnerable life situations hone their capacities for critical consciousness and agency against oppressive circuits of power?* Today, as in Baker's time, the effects of extreme poverty—hunger, chronic disease, and economic precarity—are traumatizing people across the globe, while emerging threats from the effects of climate change loom large as catastrophe after catastrophe displaces whole communities (Goldenberg, 2014). Developing a critical consciousness about those conditions and their root causes is one of many responses and perhaps often not the first or obvious one. Catalyzing leadership is based on the capacity to discern the seeds of critical consciousness in a community. Sometimes that capacity for discernment comes from outside the community. Leadership for social justice and social impact often involves a collective of differently resourced allies from inside and outside communities. Therefore, two other questions, related to the first, are required: *What critical self-reflexive work can activists from outside of communities do to prepare themselves to work with people in oppressed communities?* Allies from outside communities often are situated differently in socioeconomic strata. Baker's thinking about class distinctions was clear: there should be no distinction when it comes to democratizing access to freedom struggles. In her time, as they are today, allies from outside communities were called to check personal privilege and understand what implicit biases, assumptions, and micropractices flow from them so as not to create conditions that can block participation. Allies from outside communities also need to educate themselves about the root causes of those conditions, such as White supremacy, patriarchy, and capitalism. Hence, this question: *How should students, faculty, and administrators be prepared to take into account complexities that situate organizational-community collaborations?*

In Baker's time, as now, important allies in the civil rights movement were scholar-activists and student-activist service learners attempting to intervene against community-based state violence. Then, as now, it was important for those allies to develop a critical race consciousness about power and a belief in community power to bring about change. Many participated in workshops to hone those capacities, while some learned in the field. A critical view of knowledge production challenges hierarchical views of knowledge and expertise. By this view, knowledge comes from life experiences and not exclusively from formal education and degrees. Critical race and feminist consciousness theories are about making connections between the personal and the political—and usually there are people in oppressed communities who have already made those

connections as they have labored to fight inequities, drawing on genera-
tions of community knowledge. They need resources to support their
efforts—and not saviors.

Baker understood that naming problems through storytelling among
empathetic listeners is one way to connect the personal and political. A
fourth question for analysis is: *What motivates individuals to join social
justice organizing efforts?* In Baker's time, as now, people across the world
had the opportunity to join (or not) direct action campaigns and other social
justice efforts that may have put them in harm's way or at odds with family
and friends.[14] Intrinsic (versus extrinsic or coerced) motivation to join any
endeavor is ultimately connected to a person's deep-seated desire and an
opportunity or clear path to achieve some measure of that desire (House,
1996). The case study presented in this book focuses on youth, as did Ella
Baker at the height of her organizing career. Indeed, teenagers and young
adults have engaged in activism throughout history, even if the platforms of
that activism have changed. Even so, youth culture has always been multi-
variate, as have its routes to activism. This leads to a fifth question: *What
would truly participative spaces look like, where productive knowledge could
emerge from all angles?* Catalyzing leadership seeks to build participative
spaces where routes to collective consciousness take hold and flourish.

A sixth question: *Is it possible for a collective (not just a group of individuals) to heed the call of prefigurative politics—to "be the change we want to see
in the world"?* Prefigurative politics is a social movement strategy that
involves using methods that reflect the desired future society as captured in
Gandhi's words. In Baker's time, as now, there was a vision of society as a
participative democracy based on social equality. Then, as now, the call was
for "freedom schools" and other liberatory spaces that allow people to engage
in a *radical rehearsal* for confronting power, and also for practicing the
norms of participatory democracy, such as shared leadership, transparency,
and accountability toward commitments to social justice (Payne, 1989).

The final questions for analysis are related to social impact: *How do communities develop into "storytelling" communities of resistance to create
counternarratives to the stock stories that circulate in and around them?
Where are the places for people living under the heel of oppression to narrate
the details of their lives as a way of disrupting and transforming state-
corporate power?* In 1964, Ella Baker was one of the cofounders with Fannie

Lou Hamer and her protégé, Bob Moses, of the Mississippi Democratic Freedom Party, which managed to mobilize masses of Black people in Mississippi for a symbolic freedom ballot after they were denied voting rights in the Democratic primary election (Umoja et al., 2018).[15] Though it incurred great costs, that action and those that followed were essential in turning the tide toward the passage of the 1965 Voting Rights Act. Then, as now, that kind of broad social impact—and just as important, broadening areas of local impact—was possible through catalyzing work that engages community power and supports individual routes to collective consciousness. This book engages with these eight questions with a contemporary case analysis of a university-community collaboration.

OVERVIEW OF THE BOOK

Chapter 1, "Translating Ella Baker's Legacy of Social Justice Leadership in Everyday Praxis," situates Baker's praxis in historical context and describes more fully her catalytic leadership approach. This chapter also introduces bridge leadership as an important perspective for scholar-activists and other allies who enter communities to do social justice work. Bridge leaders such as Ella Baker are connectors in a community, most often women steeped in richly woven relational networks of kin (Stack, 1975). They often are well-informed conduits of indigenous traditions of organizing, such as the antiracist and antisexist activism that emerged from Black communities in the United States and elsewhere in the middle decades of the twentieth century (Hine et al., 1995). As explained in chapter 1 and illustrated in subsequent chapters, *catalytic social justice leadership* is a social learning process that adheres to specific participative commitments and practices that tend both to individual and relational contexts. In organizational-community collaborations to advance social justice, those commitments and practices unfold as collaborations are entered, engaged, and catalyzed. The remaining chapters are meant as a guide for applying these commitments in practice.

Chapters 2, 3, and 4 present three participative commitments of entering, engaging, and catalyzing in Baker's catalytic leadership approach. The title of each of these chapters includes a quote from Baker that encapsulates the meaning of the respective commitment. These chapters draw on data from the case study to illustrate the commitments in practice. Chapter 2, "'People Under the Heels of Oppression Should Be the Ones Leading': Entering into Community Partnerships," presents two short vignettes from the case study to illustrate the first foundational commitment of Baker's organizing praxis. She believed firmly that people living under the heels of oppression had a right "to be the ones to decide what action they were going to take to get from under their oppression " (Baker cited in Cantarow, 1980, p. 84). This commitment is important because when organizational elites enter into communities, professionalization and other claims to unique authority and knowledge often obscure community expertise. Moreover, people living with and through the trauma of oppression may be reluctant to enter into organizing relationships across boundaries of difference because of a lack of trust, a tendency to "other," and the construction of labels such as "at risk youth" (Block, 2008). This chapter asks, as Ella Baker did, how those mindsets can be revealed and countered, taking into account the conditions that produced them. The focus is on building communication capacities for critical self-reflexivity, radical listening, and networking for social justice knowledge as preconditions for participative decision-making in social justice leadership. In the catalyzing leadership approach, questioning roles, checking privilege, and orienting budding partnerships to connect community experts and those outside the community are all necessary practices for building trust and establishing a sense of belonging and accountability.

Chapter 3 delineates the communication capacity behind the second foundational commitment in Baker's approach: the maintenance of tenaciously participative decision structures. The chapter invites readers to consider how a particular context can influence the capacity for building truly participative spaces in which people can find their voices as agents of change. In our case, it reveals some of the daily struggles facing Black girls from underresourced communities as they encounter things that enable or silence their voices as agents of social change. The chapter identifies practices that the collective used to create and sustain fluid participative communication structures. It shows how girls' efforts to find their personal routes to collective consciousness were hindered or aided by allies, including adult mentors and student-service learners. Vignettes from the collective's youth-led projects illustrate communicative practices that support the second foundational commitment.

Chapter 4 exposes the workings of social power to catalyze broader impact, the third foundational commitment in Baker's approach to social justice leadership. The chapter conceptualizes social justice storytelling as a form of direct action that has the potential to expand political and economic impact. This chapter describes critical pedagogies for creating and sharing stories of coming to consciousness about structural power, healing from trauma, and implementing resistance strategies that, when deployed strategically, can expose the workings of structural power. The chapter identifies problems of communicative contexts for storytelling and how Ella Baker's philosophy of praxis reveals the possibilities and frameworks for intervention. It is about communities emerging as counter-storytelling communities, capable of narrating their own stories with political power (Bell, 2010). It is also about finding outlets for stories. Where are they shared and in what context? When do stories have the most impact for moving a community, a nation, or the world toward social justice action? Four vignettes support this chapter's theme, reflecting the multiple ways we attempted to catalyze storytelling. The first is the Harm Free Zones project that grew out of our collective's study of restorative justice. This was a community-wide initiative intended to fight the prison industrial complex. The second includes an S3! leader's deployment of her "conversion story" as part of our collective's work on the Raise the Age (RTA) Campaign, which resisted the state practice of locking up sixteen- and seventeen-year-old children in adult jails, even for minor offenses. The third and fourth vignettes widen our networks through the Comics Speak! and Youth Bridging Cultures projects.

Chapter 5, "Rewriting Ella Baker's Daybook: Integrating Self-Care and Activist Work," shifts the focus from the catalytic leadership practices explored in previous chapters to the demands of scholar-activist work to promote social justice. The chapter explores radical self-care (Lorde, 2006) in the context of scholarship-activism.

·   ·   ·   ·   ·

Perhaps after reading this introduction you're wondering about the opening quote and the reference to the "eternal struggle" for social justice.

Perhaps you are asking yourself, *What can I do to carry on the tradition Baker was passing on?* If you are a communication scholar, maybe you are wondering, *How can I apply catalytic leadership in my research and analysis?* Or if you are an activist you might be wondering, *How can I start using these practices in my work?* Or if you are a practitioner, you may be asking, *How can I use this to build capacity of volunteers in my not-for-profit organization?* These are precisely the questions that are taken up in the following chapters.

1 Translating Ella Baker's Legacy of Social Justice Leadership into Everyday Praxis

> I have always thought what is needed is the development of people who are interested not in being leaders as much as in developing leadership among other people.

Ella Baker (1972, p. 352)

When then presidential candidate Barack Obama was preparing for the 2008 Democratic primaries in South Carolina, Anton Gunn, "a self-confident young community organizer," told Mr. Obama's campaign strategists in Chicago that if they wanted to win in South Carolina, they should enlist the "'[Ms.] Mary's,' older women who were centers of good will and polite gossip in the black churches, who had a hand in every charity event and Bible-study group" (Remnick, 2015, p. 26). The strategists heeded that advice. Candidate Obama went on to win the primary by a landslide over challengers Hillary Clinton and John Edwards ("Election 2008," 2016). I do not mean to suggest that Black women were the *only* reason Obama won in South Carolina, but they were certainly a factor, as they have been in more recent political races (Bowerman, 2017). But Gunn's reference to the "Ms. Marys" in a community does speak to the organizing tradition of bridge leadership in Black women's history, a historical tradition of organizing that can be traced (at least) back to antiracist resistance to chattel slavery in the United States and that found traction during the twentieth-century movements for education reform, civil rights, and protections against sexual violence (Robnett, 1996). It is a tradition of leadership that has been passed on through carriers, such as Ella Baker and others throughout the world, who believed, as exemplified in the opening quote, in the development of social justice leadership in other people (Baker, 1972; Parker, 2004; Payne, 1995/2007).

This chapter translates Ella Baker's philosophy into everyday praxis. It connects Black women's bridge leadership to critical organizing concepts advanced by the Italian philosopher Antonio Gramsci (1891–1937). In her comprehensive biography of Baker, Barbara Ransby made a similar comparison. Her intent was *not* to somehow legitimize Ella Baker's ideas by likening them to those of a European philosopher, as some critics have alleged (Ransby, 2003).[1] Rather, she argued persuasively that such comparisons necessarily write Black women's intellectual thought back into the academic canons that have erased and ignored them. Positioning Black women's intellectual history within the context of other ideas, Ransby observed, subverts the tendency to "essentialize and isolate black thought from parallel ideologies" (2003, p. 419). It also expands intellectual thought. Antonio Gramsci was born only twelve years before Ella Baker, making them contemporaries at the height of his political engagement: Gramsci in southern Italy in the 1920s and 1930s, under Mussolini's fascist regime, and Baker in Depression-era Harlem, New York, later in the Jim Crow South, and finally in global antiracist movements. Gramsci died as a political prisoner at a relatively young age and therefore was unable to fully test his ideas in the field.[2] Over more than fifty years, from 1929 until her death in 1986, Ella Baker was able to experiment with and develop a social justice praxis that was similar in theory and practice to Gramsci's philosophy of praxis. As Ransby has suggested, centering Ella Baker's approach within the Gramscian tradition might provoke new ways of thinking about now-familiar Gramscian concepts.

Here I advance Ransby's analysis to illustrate how Ms. Baker's praxis illuminates, racializes, and extends several of Gramsci's ideas (see also Wilderson, 2003) and applies to bridge leadership in community organizing.[3] The chapter then discusses three commitments that underlie Ella Baker's catalytic leadership approach. Those commitments are translated into the context of organization-community partnerships and the corresponding communication practices that people can use to tackle problems as they work together for social justice (see table 1).

Table 1 Three Commitments for Catalytic Leadership
Problems and Communication Practices

Chapter	Commitment	Problem	Communication Practices
Chapter 2: Entering into Community Partnerships—"People under the heels of oppression should be the ones leading." (Baker, 1980)	1st: commitment to community power	**Voice:** obstacles to community expertise in defining problems, co-constructing interventions, and leading action	• Critical self-reflexivity: questioning roles; checking privilege • Radical listening for entering partnerships: listening as intentionality toward coaction • Critical networking: convening spaces of fellowship in which community experts and academic/other sources of expertise commingle to build trust and mutual respect and identify social justice needs
Chapter 3: Creating Participative Spaces for Social Justice Organizing—"Think in radical terms." (Baker, 1969/1999)	2nd: commitment to group-centered leadership	**Participation:** problems of hierarchical difference that thwart the strategic use of different kinds of power/ knowledge resources	• Radical listening for creating "free spaces": listening for context; listening for silences; listening for multiple angles of vision • Critical dialogic group structure and processes: group facilitation capacities for everyone; discussions about different forms of expertise; mutual learning structures that support trial and error; circle processes that encourage dialogue; rotating leadership roles • Participative decision-making: tilted toward the least powerful when there are threats to humanity
Chapter 4: Engaging Social Justice Storytelling for Catalytic Leadership—"Strong people don't need strong leaders." (Baker 1980)	3rd: commitment to exposing the workings of structural power	**Broader impact:** problems of coalition building to realize political and economic impact	• Critical pedagogies for creating counter-storytelling communities: storytelling for social justice framework; coactive service learning classrooms; popular education/performance • Joining or creating coactive spaces for social justice storytelling: convening conferences; hosting forums; creating counter-storytelling art

Ella Baker has been called a Gramscian "organic intellectual" (Ransby, 2003). Gramsci understood organic intellectuals as people who are "in the know" about how power circulates to create inequity in civil society (analytics) and who can translate everyday knowledge within oppressed communities into a collective political narrative to advance social justice (mechanisms for popular education).[4] Baker also has been called a "radical whose genius was her ability to develop democratic and activist political organizations and communities" (Omolade, 1994, p. 164). These two descriptors, organic intellectual and organizing genius, are both good ones for Ella Baker's praxis, and they also convey key connections between Baker's and Gramsci's philosophies, although there are differences as well. Both Baker and Gramsci emphasized the necessity of analyses that define how oppressive power is working in the current historical moment as well as concrete mechanisms for social justice change tactics that flow from those analytics (see also Hall, 1987; Kipfer 2008). From this perspective, not all "Ms. Marys" in a community are organic intellectuals, but those who *are* have the potential to educate and catalyze others to build social movements. Often they are the well-informed carriers of indigenous traditions of organizing. What "bridge leaders" mostly have in common is knowledge about who is in the community, the history of the community, and the dynamics of "what's going on," to recall Marvin Gaye's popular phrase, and how these arrangements of "goings on" produce culture.

Bridge leaders inside a community are not "informants" in the usual ethnographic sense; rather, they are *community experts*, with various levels of consciousness about organizing strategy, who become allies in discovering and defining catalyzing questions or social change problems. They work closely with allies outside the community to mobilize resources to carry out the research or social justice action. Often organic intellectuals come from outside the community to connect with and provide the space to develop their full potential for those who are already, or in the process of becoming, organic intellectuals.

Ella Baker was an organic intellectual allied with people in communities; like Gramsci, she believed that organic intellectuals existed within the spaces where people are living through oppression. She gained that perspective at a young age from people living in her community of origin.

Raised in rural Littleton, North Carolina, in the Jim Crow South of the early 1900s, her activism was anchored within the Black freedom struggle, born out of "a political analysis that recognized the historical significance of racism as the cornerstone of an unjust social and economic order in the United States" (Ransby, 2003, p. 5). Baker's historical analysis informed a working theory of broad social transformation based on the idea of exposing the bankrupt claims of White supremacy, capitalism, and patriarchy. She saw those systems as the often-uninterrogated root causes of economic exploitation, marginalization from the political process, and other oppressive conditions faced by African Americans and other groups in the United States and around the world. From her enslaved grandmother, whose personal resistance to White terror got her demoted from the "big house" to the "fields," to her mother's activism through the Black church, Baker's family and community instilled in her a tradition of questioning and resisting those systems in many ways and at many levels.

Gramsci's questioning of oppressive political systems emerged out of strife and struggle in ways that distinguished him from other prominent European philosophers. He was born in the backwoods of Sardinia in southern Italy but later attended the University of Turin on a scholarship for poor students from his area (Buttigieg, 1972/2011 Vol. 1, p. 66). He struggled his entire life with a debilitating illness, exacerbated by political persecution. Though he is now among the most noted continental philosophers, Gramsci is the only one among them with that distinctive background (Ekers et al., 2012). From a young age he honed a socialist analysis and Marxist critique of the rich and powerful; later, while in college, he was impressed by the mass participation of peasants in political life. In the late 1920s, he was just beginning to gain traction in testing out a praxis to integrate political and economic action with popular cultural activity when illness and political imprisonment intervened. He died in 1937 after years of what biographer Buttigieg described as "excruciating physical deterioration, devastating loneliness, and profound anguish" (1972/2011, Vol. 1, p. 2).

Gramsci was never able to fully test his method for an *antidogmatic philosophy of praxis*, which he developed while writing from his cell as a political prisoner under Mussolini's fascist regime. However, like Baker, Gramsci has inspired activists around the world who seek a praxis of concrete, community-based knowledge and historically informed strategies for social justice.

.   .   .   .   .

Baker's and Gramsci's analyses are unified especially in their attention to two questions: Under what conditions do people in vulnerable life situations develop consciousness and agency against oppression, and relatedly, what histories of knowledge production about social change should guide those who attempt to ally with these people?

In addition to the concept of the organic intellectual, other Gramscian concepts undergirding these questions are *subalternity*, *hegemony* and *manufacturing consent*, and *common sense* (*senso commune*) and *good sense* (*buon senso*). Each of these concepts resonates in Baker's philosophy. If you are working as a social justice activist or planning to do so, consider how these concepts and their application might translate to your work.

Like Gramsci's, Baker's vision of a radical plural democracy remained tenaciously inclusive of the concrete, lived experiences of masses of people living under the heels of oppression. Gramsci's concept of the subaltern is the idea that historical, economic, political, and cultural contexts are continually shaping people's lives, exiling some to the margins of civil society. Within these subaltern spaces Gramsci saw both the workings of oppressive power and resistance to it (Golding, 1992). Likewise, Baker understood the importance of subaltern spaces to creatively resist power. However, unlike Gramsci's organizing philosophy, Baker's was informed by her lived experience with White supremacy as it permeates communities of color. A Bakerian theory of subalternity, I argue, recognizes White supremacist-capitalistic-driven terror as a root cause of many different kinds of oppression. Baker's analysis centered on community expertise and people's capacities to name that terror in sociocultural political terms and fight for a new social arrangement rooted in liberty for all. She explained her philosophy thus: "In order for us as poor and oppressed people to become a part of a society that is meaningful, the system under which we now exist has to be radically changed. This means that we are going to have to learn to think in radical terms. I use the term radical in its original meaning—getting down to and understanding the root cause. It means facing a system that does not lend itself to your needs and devising a means by which you change that system" (quoted in Ransby, 2003, p. 1).

Like Baker, Gramsci was concerned with the roots of power. He saw the capitalist state as a hegemonic (dominant) power made up of two overlapping spheres of ruling relations: a political society and a civil society. A political society is ruled through the enforcement of laws, policies, and regulations. In contrast, a civil society is ruled through everyday norms reproduced in cultural life—for example, through the media, universities, and religious institutions. Gramsci understood that hegemony was most effectively reproduced via cultural life, wherein the state could "'manufacture consent' and legitimacy" (Heywood, 1994, pp. 100–101). Oppressive hegemonic power is at the height of its effectiveness when civil society reproduces "commonsense" norms that lead people to unwittingly defend the very systems that are oppressing them and others.[5]

Like Gramsci, Baker understood that oppressive hegemony could be reconfigured as a liberating hegemony, converting common sense into good sense through an interrogation of the root causes of economic exploitation and marginalization from the political process. However, she understood that that interrogation needs to be grounded in the concrete, and it must be informed by the historical context of people's lives. Baker was a staunch believer in the creation of "free spaces" where people could have the openness and safety to question commonsense understandings. Free spaces may begin in the places where people tend to gather out of cultural habit: at beauty shops, at church functions, or after school. However, the introduction of critical pedagogy—a workshop on protection against violence, citizenship education, or a call to historical memory through arts activism—can transform that beauty shop into a space for building a liberating hegemony.

For example, Baker played a role in the formation of cooperatives in the 1930s, "freedom schools" in the 1960s, and the Mississippi Democratic Freedom Party in the 1960s and into the 1970s (see figure 1). These are all examples of her lifelong commitment to the importance of free radical spaces in a plural democracy (see Ransby, 2003). She was able to elaborate the critical art of finding the adequate practical form of her theory (Barge, 2006). Baker differed from Gramsci because she shared the lived experience with the people with whom she worked, as a raced and gendered body. This is not to minimize Gramsci's experience and suffering.

Figure 1. Ella Baker addressing Mississippi Freedom Democratic Party delegates at boardwalk rally during Democratic National Convention in Atlantic City, NJ, August 10, 1964. Photo from 1976 George Ballis/Take Stock.

Imprisoned by Mussolini's fascist regime for over a decade, he witnessed firsthand what happens to people who are incarcerated, the "molecular changes" that they themselves often do not notice. Gramsci did notice that those changes were happening to him. He gave "losing the ability to laugh at myself" as one example (Gramsci, 1993, p. 233). But at the same time, that knowledge of the lives of the incarcerated did not seem to be central to Gramsci's ideas about common sense. I think there is something to the notion of empathizing with the common sense already existing in a collective that allows us to lead a critique of that common sense. That capacity to empathize with, and simultaneously critique, common sense is what I think Ella Baker had, and it was a quality that she never lost. She never lost sight of the practical form of the theory that could lead to a radical knowledge of how history was determining the present. This legacy lives on in a community power–based, catalyzing approach to leadership.

Crehan has cautioned, however, that coming to terms with a subaltern existence, and the good sense/*buon senso* that emerges out of that process, should not "gloss over the complicated dialectical relationship between 'precepts of folk wisdom' and developed and coherent political philosophies" (2016, p. 48). Both Gramsci and Baker understood that not all responses to subalternity would contribute to transformative change to radical democracy. Instead, both were skeptical about any forms of organizing based on the premise that existing hierarchical power relations were the only ones possible. "Strong people don't need strong leaders" (Cantarow, 1980, p. 53) was Baker's critique of oppressive state power, and it was also a critique of a kind of charismatic leadership that relied on individual personalities. She advanced those critiques in her professional associations with social movement organizations, including the National Association for the Advancement of Colored People (NAACP). Founded in 1909, the NAACP is one of the oldest and most influential civil rights organizations in the United States. Significantly, throughout the 1940s, when Baker was serving as a field secretary and later as director of branches, the NAACP grew exponentially. In 1946, it had nearly 600,000 members (NAACP, n.d.). In that year Baker left the organization, frustrated that her criticism of the top-down bureaucratic leadership of the organization had gone unheeded. Baker believed in community power: organic intellectuals who emerged from networks built through a critique of racial, patriarchal, and capitalistic systems. She drew on a tradition steeped in bridge leadership.

Bridge leadership is a process of grassroots mobilization that links people in different communities and social movements, such as those advancing labor and educational reforms, civil rights, environmental justice, and protections against sexual violence (Robnett, 1996). As those movements take shape, they are usually represented in popular culture by a few visible and vocal leaders. Often the people most affected by the social justice policies that these movements hope to achieve are left behind, while their contributions and, importantly, their interests are diminished or, worse, reconstituted to serve other interests (Fine & Weis, 1998). As Hall points out (following Gramsci), "Interests are not given, but have to be politically and ideologically constructed" (1987, p. 20; see also Clarke, 2015). Bridge leadership addresses that concern. It forms an intermediate layer of leadership that is relational and rooted in communities—in the places, people, and conversations where ideological work can take place and be sustained over time. Specifically, bridge leadership provides connections between

(a) *social movement organizations* [e.g., unions and other advocacy groups] and *potential constituents* [e.g., people in repressive work organizations and other oppressed communities];

(b) *prefigurative politics* [enacting a vision of a just world—Occupy Wall Street (OWS), for example] and *strategic politics* [mandates for strategic interventions—OWS has been critiqued for not having these kinds of mandates; see Smucker, 2014];[6] and

(c) *potential leaders* [people seeking change] and *those already predisposed to movement activity* [people leading change, often under siege and under resourced]. (Robnett, 1996, p. 1661, emphasis added)

The learn-teach-lead method of leadership communication defines Baker's praxis as one that catalyzes personal routes to collective consciousness and provides a blueprint for collective leadership action. We can now connect the learn-teach-lead method, described in this book's introduction, to Baker's bridge leadership. In this view, Ella Baker's bridge leadership is about catalyzing hope and possibility in the face of totalizing power structures. Baker understood the temporal and spatial demands of that work, as is clear in her assertion that "the struggle is eternal. Somebody else carries on" (Cantarow, 1980, p. 93). This was not an assertion that the work of social justice is futile, but rather that it is ongoing. It is highly contextual and shot through with history that (re)appears in the present. In other words, there will always be a need for analysis of how oppressive hegemony is reasserting itself. Baker's approach to bridge leadership—through learning, teaching, and leading—maintains the seeds of resistance to oppressive power *and* the mechanisms through which people can remain connected to movements for social justice.

·   ·   ·   ·   ·

For Ella Baker, like bridge leaders who came before her in the United States, resistance was rooted historically in resistance to White supremacist, capitalistic, and patriarchal systems. These interlocking forms of oppression had persisted for centuries and permeated the lifeworld of Black and Brown people globally. Beginning as early as the 1600s and continuing to the present day, Black women in the United States have immersed themselves in their communities—and in people's suffering—to find opportunities for organized social justice resistance. We have answered the call to organize against sexual violence, connected with and started (slavery and prison) abolitionist movements (especially those grounded in education reforms), and pursued opportunities for economic empowerment (Giddings, 1984; Gilkes, 1980; Hine et al., 1995; McGuire, 2010).

The lifeworlds—immediate experiences, activities, and associations—of women and girls in communities provide important spaces for bridge leadership and for seeding social justice movements that connect intersectionally and globally to other liberation movements. These spaces are where the common sense of survival can be transformed into the good sense of resistance and transformation. For example, Black women immersed in the suffering of enslaved communities of the US antebellum South found creative ways to organize against sexual violence (Hine et al., 1995).[7] The sexual exploitation of Black women by White men is one of the horrific legacies of US chattel slavery that continued through the last decades of the twentieth century (McGuire, 2010). Interracial rape was used to uphold White patriarchal power and was part of a larger apparatus of racial and sexual violence and terror that deployed coercion, control, and harassment (Hall, 1983). Black women bridge leaders such as Ella Baker, Rosa Parks, and countless others who came before and after them honed their activist capacities in the struggle to end violence against Black women. Whether that violence was physical or psychological, and whether it was advanced through individual, systemic, or institutional means, these women worked with various forms of radical storytelling, personal protest, and organized action to catalyze others and change the status quo (McGuire, 2010).[8]

Harriet Jacobs's autobiography, which included vivid details of her experiences with slaveholder lechery, is one antebellum example of radical storytelling to catalyze action. Jacobs's aim was to "arouse the women of the North" and "convince the people of the Free States what Slavery really is" (McGuire, 2010, p. xviii). Reconstruction-era Black women activists, such as Ida B. Wells, Anna Julia Cooper, and myriad networks of Black clubwomen, worked in local, national, and international circles to protest violence against Black women (Lerner, 1974; McGuire, 2010, p. xviii).

Through personal resolve, an analysis of the collective suffering of Black people, and an understanding of threats to human liberty, they created platforms for protest speeches. Most notably, Ida B. Wells, a journalist and human and civil rights activist from Memphis, Tennessee, traveled nationally and internationally to cultivate moral indignation against American lynching (Gordon Nembhard, 2014; Wells-Barnett, 1892/2012). She also spoke out against "the rape of helpless Negro girls, which began in slavery days, [and] still continues without reproof from church, state, or press" (Giddings, 1984, p. 31).

Ella Baker and her contemporaries in the twentieth century built upon this legacy of antiracist feminist resistance. In 1935, Baker wrote about and protested against the sexual violence and economic exploitation of Black women domestic workers in New York. She and her coauthor, Marvel Cooke, went undercover to learn firsthand about the workings of what they called the "Bronx slave market" and then wrote about it in what might have been on a par with today's *Huffington Post*, the NAACP's flagship magazine, the *Crisis*. Baker and Cooke called for labor organizing that took into account the root causes that sustained the exploitation of day labor: "(1) the general ignorance of and apathy towards organized labor action; (2) the artificial barriers that separate the interest of the relief administrators and investigators from that of their 'case loads,' the white collar and professional worker from the laborer and the domestic; and (3) organized labor's limited concept of exploitation, which permits it to fight vigorously to secure itself against evil, yet passively or actively aids and abets the ruthless destruction of [Black people]" (1935, p. 340). True to Baker's philosophy of excavating and catalyzing community-based power, the *Crisis* article reported on how the women of the market were already attacking some of these root causes. Specifically, it described "an embryonic labor union [that] now exists in the Simpson avenue 'mart.' Girls who persist in working for less than thirty cents an hour have been literally run off the corner" (p. 340). The article provided an example of a recent action in which women "of the 'mart' actually demanded and refused to work for less than thirty-five cents an hour" (p. 340). Baker and Cook amplified these women's actions across the broad readership of the *Crisis*.

Civil rights campaigns in what would become hotspots of resistance in the South—Little Rock, Arkansas; Macon, Georgia; Tallahassee,

Florida; Washington, North Carolina; Birmingham and Selma, Alabama; Hattiesburg, Mississippi; and many other places—had roots in organized resistance to sexual violence and appeals for protection of Black womanhood. Rosa Parks was "a militant race woman, a sharp detective, and an antirape activist long before she became the patron saint of the [1955 Montgomery, Alabama] bus boycott" (McGuire, 2010, p. xvii). In 1944, after meeting with Recy Taylor, a young mother who had been raped at gunpoint by White men in Abbeville, Alabama, Rosa Parks worked with local people to form the Committee for Equal Justice. As McGuire explained: "Eleven years later this group of homegrown leaders would become better known as the Montgomery Improvement Association. The 1955 Montgomery bus boycott, often heralded as the opening scene of the civil rights movement, was in many ways the last act of a decades-long struggle to protect black women, like Taylor, from sexualized violence and rape" (2010, p. xvii). Bridge leadership starts at the level of the personal and the small group, to nurture the seeds of social justice organizing. It connects people and movements when the time is right to do so.

·　　·　　·　　·　　·

Through her analysis of gender in the US Civil Rights Movement, Robnett illustrated how bridge leadership was accomplished through communication strategies, such as framing, amplification, extension, and transformation, to connect prefigurative and strategic politics (1996, p. 1680). These are the primary tools that help communities move from a common sense about how things are to a good sense about how things could be. Prefigurative politics is about consciousness-raising, identity, and change. It is extraordinary work, in the sense that ordinary people come to exhibit a kind of courage that previously may have seemed unimaginable to them. Consider, for example, the transformation required for tenant farmers in the Jim Crow South of the 1950s to risk what little material goods they had, and their lives, to vote, as happened in Fayetteville, Tennessee; McComb, Mississippi; and other places. Where did a teenaged woman in Mississippi find the courage to join the fight for freedom amid the violence of the early 1960s, as did young women in the Student Nonviolent Coordinating Committee (SNCC) such as Hellen O'Neal-McCray, who defied not only segregationist authorities but also her family to join the dangerous direct-action campaigns of the Civil Rights Movement (Holsaert et al., 2010)?

Bridge leadership is a process for discovering from the grassroots the knowledge of what *is* possible. Ella Baker understood that that kind of knowledge is found in subaltern spaces: in the silences, paradoxes, resistance to, and decision to take action that emerge from those with their necks under the heels of power and injustice (Ransby, 2003). She first began working out the specifics of that perspective in the 1930s, when she immersed herself in and was an influencer on what she later described as "a hotbed of radical thinking" in Harlem (Cantarow, 1980, p. 64). Writing and engaging in intellectual debates, she helped forge the rapidly developing cooperative movement for economic empowerment during the worst years of the Great Depression.

In the 1940s, working as the NAACP director of branches, she applied that knowledge, laying the groundwork for the coming Black freedom movements in the South by reframing the ways local branches engaged with national organizations. For example, instead of engaging in the normal practice of simply asking members of local branches to pay dues and receive dignitaries, Baker trained local people to become leaders. She organized and taught a series of workshops in which she honed her group-centered leadership approach. And she arranged for people to collect their stories of resistance to help fuel the movement. Their everyday acts of resistance and martyrdom in the Jim Crow South had been part of a quiet, hidden struggle for survival—one that suddenly found new meaning as fuel for a growing national freedom movement.

Ella Baker's efforts to reframe community members' experiences as essential to a growing national freedom movement was also a form of amplification and extension. Local resistance to violence against Black bodies and the fight for voting rights, which were already well under way in certain circles, intensified as the *cause du jour*. These efforts were rearticulated and extended to new recruits through local grassroots leadership within local NAACP branches. By many accounts, Baker's intellectual engagement and prodding later made a great difference in those years of rapid transformation from 1960 to 1964, when all she had been working out—her interpretation of those fragments of a leadership tradition over decades—suddenly found a perfect testing ground among young activists who would become the SNCC.

Bridge leadership, then, is a listening process. People trained in the critical pedagogies of movement building, immersed in communities, must first be attuned to people's personal, organizational, and community routes to collective political action. That happens over time, and the process is not linear, as Baker's praxis demonstrates.

That praxis was based on "leadership as teaching," which puts in productive tension two traditional ideas of prebureaucratic *community organizing* and organic *group-centered leadership*. Prebureaucratic community organizing involves a focus on moving people and directing events through, for example, policy advocacy training on themes such as convening meetings, public speaking, and the use of social media. In contrast, Baker's philosophy of group-centered leadership focuses on creating "the social space necessary for . . . oppressed people . . . to speak and act on their own behalf" (Ransby, 2003, p. 45). Leadership as teaching is about the creation and cultivation of organic intellectuals *from the grassroots* up and not from the top down. It incorporates time-tested organizing pedagogies for communication advocacy, but these pedagogies are not an end in themselves; rather, the focus is on meeting people where they are, taking into account their context of oppression, and facilitating personal routes to collective consciousness and mobilized action. Leadership as teaching is an approach that "changes the nature of what it means to be successful. How many people show up for a rally may matter less than how much the people who organize the rally learn from doing so" (Payne, 1989, p. 892). Learning the mechanics of organizing, growing in self-confidence, and developing interpersonal bonds in the fight for social justice happen in participative spaces where people feel that they belong and can hold each other accountable for their social justice efforts.

.   .   .   .   .

Even when potential allies are intentional about organizing with people in communities and engaging with local knowledge, their efforts may be plagued by problems that can seem insurmountable. Baker's group-centered, catalyzing leadership approach provides guidance for confronting those problems and pursuing commitments to social justice collaborations. Table 1 outlines three problems that correlate to the three commitments in Ella Baker's catalyzing leadership approach: voice, participation, and broadening social impact. Each of these commitments and corresponding problems is summarized in the following discussion, along with the communication practices for learning, teaching, and leading social justice action. They are further elaborated on in subsequent chapters.

The first commitment to catalytic leadership is to the belief that "people under the heels of oppression should be the ones leading" (Cantarow, 1980, p. 84). Catalytic leadership in this instance addresses the problems of *voice* that are most salient when organization-community partnerships are first being formed. The most important charge is to identify obstacles to community expertise in defining problems, co-constructing interventions, and leading action (Dempsey & Barge, 2014). These are the major problems of subalternity, discussed further in chapter 2.

The communication practices that help address these problems start with an intentional acknowledgment of the power dynamics that exist in organization-community partnerships. Specifically, they flow from *critical self-reflexivity*, *critical networking*, and *radical listening*. Critical self-reflexivity involves using critical pedagogies—writing, performance, and art—to actively and publicly acknowledge and challenge how power and privilege are operating in ourselves and in organization-community partnerships. This can be a deeply transformative experience if attended to with empathy and within the context of a commitment to community power. It is also a knowledge production process that lays the groundwork for moving from common sense to good sense as people begin to see the critical assets that each person brings to the collective's social justice aims. Critical networking goes beyond self-interested socializing to convening spaces of fellowship that connect community experts and academic or other sources of expertise. This is the community building that begins before partnerships can be formed. Critical networking occurs in spaces where bridge leaders discern whether community interests and expertise are acknowledged in the first place among those outside the community who say they have come to support their social justice causes. These are spaces in which to build trust and mutual respect and to identify social justice needs.

Radical listening is the capacity to take full account of the context of structural inequality that might hinder people from seeing their own power to change things. Especially at the point of entry into partnerships, radical listening involves being intentional about coaction, in which individuals enact the capacity for empathy (Follett, 1924). If a person is not showing up at a meeting, for example, or not speaking up, then radical listening would spark a curiosity about what led to that absence or that reluctance to speak, rather than a judgment about not meeting a particular time commitment or failing to follow rules and protocols. Radical listening means staying attuned to personal routes to collective action and creating a space for those routes to develop.

.   .   .   .   .

The second commitment is toward implementing participative practices that cultivate and nurture voices in a productive dialectical process. It is a commitment to both a process and content. Specifically, the commitment is to use participative decision-making processes and structures that tilt toward the least powerful in society (Payne, 1989). This commitment means implementing critical dialogic group structures and processes—for example, mutual learning structures, as opposed to hierarchical ones, that support trial and error; circular processes that encourage dialogue; and rotating leadership roles that decenter individual power. Another key relational capacity is participative decision-making. However, participative decision-making within asymmetrical power arrangements—especially those contextualized by race—can only be sustained if joined to a commitment to radical listening in free spaces, where people know that they can speak up and be heard. Each of these three processes contributes to knowledge production intended to build a liberating hegemony from the ground up.

.   .   .   .   .

The third and final commitment is to exposing the workings of structural power through counter-storytelling communities (Bell, 2010). Counter-storytelling communities resist the narratives and labels placed on them from outside (Bell, 2010; Block, 2008). Labels such as "crime infested" and "welfare queens," or "at-risk" youth and "super predators" linger in the public consciousness. They support oppressive policies about policing, education, and economic empowerment by shutting down other narratives and discourses that would defy or subvert the power structure. This kind of narrative closure is forcefully demonstrated in the rhetoric of two US presidents known for their strategic use of communication. In the 1980s, Ronald Reagan popularized the phrase "welfare queen" to target and label Black women in vulnerable communities as scapegoats when the administration enacted morally bankrupt policies that further impoverished children and enriched corporations. More recently, in 2019, Donald Trump's tweets about the predominantly Black city of Baltimore being "crime infested" and a place where "no human being would want to live" were strategically deployed to accomplish similar aims (Itkowitz, 2019).

Ella Baker's mantra that "strong people don't need strong leaders" is a testament to community power manifested in the capacity for communities to tell their *own* stories. Counter-storytelling addresses the problem of achieving *broader impact*. A crucial capacity for building social movements is to build coalitions that can have real political and economic impacts (Robnett, 1996). Storytelling for social justice is a primary vehicle for empowering organic intellectuals from all angles of vision. As I show in chapter 4, storytelling for social justice involves using the critical arts, performance, and other pedagogies for creating and sharing stories with broader audiences. A crucial part of the process involves creating spaces in which those stories can be told to expose and disrupt impacts of structural power, advance strategies to heal from trauma, and implement resistance strategies to achieve social justice outcomes (Baker, 1960; Bell, 2010).

These three commitments, together, animate the learn-teach-lead method that is a core technology of the Ella Baker Women's Center's flagship girl-centered leadership program, Striving Sisters Speak! (S3!).

2 "People Under the Heels of Oppression Should Be the Ones Leading"

ENTERING INTO COMMUNITY PARTNERSHIPS

When academic researchers, community-development organization workers, and volunteers enter communities, we might be working with, for, or even against the people living there. Sometimes we are doing all three, whether our intentions are transparent (to ourselves and others) or not. This is due to the complex power dynamics and often uninterrogated structural contexts of organization-community relations described in chapter 1.

This chapter tells the story of the beginning of my journey as a communication scholar-activist, attempting to follow Ella Baker's foundational grassroots organizing principle of believing in the power of people in communities to lead social justice actions for change: "people who [are] under the heel" of oppression have to be in the leadership when it comes to getting that heel off their necks (Ransby, 2003, p. 195). It is a story about how I grappled with the questions introduced in the last chapter and the problems of voice and the identification of obstacles to community expertise in defining problems, co-constructing interventions, and leading action. In my case, the challenge was to find my voice as a Black woman and academic researcher engaging girls and women whose experiences both intersected with and departed from my own.

Table 2 Entering into Community Partnerships
Commitment, Problem, and Communication Practices

Commitment	*Problem*	*Communication Practices*
Community power: "People under the heels [of oppression] should be the ones leading." (Baker, 1980)	**Voice:** obstacles to community expertise in defining problems, co-constructing interventions, and leading action	• Critical self-reflexivity: questioning roles; checking privilege • Radical listening for entering partnerships: listening as intentionality toward coaction • Critical networking: convening spaces of fellowship in which community experts and academic/other sources of expertise commingle to build trust and mutual respect and identify social justice needs

Relationships between the "organizer" and the "organized" are complex. As a critically conscious scholar-activist, it is instinctive to want to fight alongside people living under the heel of oppression. And as an African American woman who grew up in the segregated rural South with relatives whose ancestors had migrated to Black communities in the urban North, I felt I had the credentials—I had earned the right—to place myself alongside the residents of University Heights and Regal Gardens to do this work. I was partially wrong and partially right, and I had to learn that often it was I who was being "developed" and "organized."

This chapter presents two vignettes from the case study to illustrate the problems of subalternity in organization-community partnerships and discusses three vital communication practices necessary to advance a commitment to community power: *critical self-reflexivity* (questioning roles and checking privilege), *radical listening* (listening to silences to inform social justice work), and *networking for social justice knowledge* (convening spaces of fellowship among community experts, academics, and people with other kinds of expertise) (see table 2). A brief conceptual framing of those practices is presented next, followed by the vignettes "Holding Stories: Between Horror and Hope" and "Remaking the Rules." Each vignette concludes with some practical responses to the main question guiding this chapter's analysis: *How should people from outside communities—students, faculty, volunteers, administrators—be prepared emotionally, intellectually, and practically to take into account complexities that situate organizational-community collaborations?*

.   .   .   .   .

Ella Baker's praxis underscores that we need to develop a critical consciousness about race and privilege. As she mentored volunteers heading to the deep American South of the 1950s and 1960s, she was keenly aware that people from privileged positions outside of the communities besieged by White terror needed to develop a critical consciousness about their privilege and how they might help or harm the advancement of social justice. "Those who are well heeled don't want to get un-well-heeled," she argued. "If they are acceptable to the Establishment and they're wielding power which serves their interest, they can assume too readily that that also serves the interest of everybody."[1] Baker was actively engaged in shaping a process wherein organizers would understand the critical importance of learning from local leaders and respectfully building on that wisdom by adding whatever expertise they were bringing to the effort. Her method was twofold. First, she identified and nourished the radical democratic tendencies she saw among those attracted to the movement. For example, she personally recruited White college graduates like Mary King, who as a student organizer at Ohio Wesleyan University had demonstrated the kind of critical race consciousness in her activism that showed solidarity with Black oppression in the United States.[2] Baker also handpicked and mentored Black women college students whom she saw demonstrating radical democratic work, like Bernice Johnson Reagon and Diane Nash, and recent college graduates like Bob Moses, who in 1960 left his teaching job in New York City to join the emerging Black Freedom movement.[3] Moses became Baker's political apprentice, honing and advancing her philosophies of community-led organizing and direct action as an organizer in the early years of the SNCC, which she helped to found in 1960. Her second means for critical consciousness-raising was through education. She advocated for and helped institute critical educational programs for staff and the hundreds of student volunteers—mostly White—who were set to arrive in Mississippi for Freedom Summer in 1964. The expectation was that the volunteers would assist more experienced SNCC field staff in voter education and registration campaigns, working in communities alongside Black residents involved in the organizing efforts, while also bringing national attention to the movement and demanding accountability from the rest of the country for what happened in Mississippi (Ransby, 2003, p. 317).

To be critically self-reflexive means being attuned to historical contexts that give rise to different iterations of state- and corporate-sanctioned violence, creating what Weis and Fine termed "limit situations," in which people are striving to live in their full humanity within the limits of those structures (2013, p. 229). It also means being capable of questioning one's own complicity in structural violence, a process that the young middle-class SNCC volunteers in the 1960s—Black and White—undertook as they joined the Black Freedom movement in Mississippi and other strongholds of racism in the South. In social justice leadership studies, critical self-reflexivity is distinguished from simply being aware of one's "positionality," or the social and political context that shapes one's identity. Simply being self-aware is only a starting point. Think of a mirror large enough to reflect multiple images—yours and those of others—and the relations of awareness required to move beyond those surface images. Critical self-reflexivity is about shifting toward a deep questioning of privilege that reframes one's perspective. In community-based partnerships, it involves being able to interrogate one's privilege as well as one's complicity with structural violence advanced through racism, extreme capitalism, and militarism.

Atrocities committed by the state and private corporations alike are hidden in plain sight. They are advanced through persistent racist institutional structures that intersect with other controlling structures, such as patriarchy and heteronormativity, that together form a matrix of domination (Collins, 1990). For example, King (2014) has argued that Black labor (from enslavement to mass incarceration) is just one kind of use within an open, violent, and infinite repertoire of practices that make Black flesh fungible. Each of us, intentionally or not, helps do that work, and we each can come to terms with how we can confront and eradicate it.

Tracing the routes from past atrocities to structural causes of present inequities and new atrocities—what scholar-activists refer to as structural analysis (Hale, 2001)—is foundational to oppressive systems. It reveals the complex milieu of scholar-activists' work and complicates their capacity for structural analysis.

I entered the work at University Heights and Regal Gardens knowing that Black girls' lives exist within a world that advances the belief that Black flesh is disposable (Wilderson, 2003). I was also aware that my positioning as a faculty member at an elite university made me an outsider. At the same time, however, my Blackness enabled the potential for empathy with the girls' positionality. The time I spent in the neighborhood also contributed to a positive human connection. However, the stark reality was that I occupied a place of privilege relative to theirs. The discourses that fuel violence against the spirit by the state (deserving/undeserving, right/wrong) are also discernible in the dichotomy of privileged/less privileged. Critical self-reflexivity and deep listening were required to disrupt those discourses into the potential for partnerships for social justice leadership.

When Baker was catalyzing grassroots leadership in the Jim Crow South of the 1950s and 1960s, she was developing a method of what might be called persistent intentionality to work *with* people in communities. Her approach took full account of the context of structural inequality that might hinder people from seeing their own power to change things. At the same time, she held firmly to the belief that the fulcrum of social change was to keep local knowledge consistently in the foreground in social justice leadership. In that space—between "social truth" and "social strategy"—the work of radical listening and critical self-reflexivity is crucial.[4]

In Baker's praxis, radical listening entailed taking the time to engage the indigenous knowledge of a community. This approach is radical because it goes beyond the rational norm of listening, which entails speaking-hearing-processing-responding. Instead, radical listening involves listening for the seeds of becoming: people from all angles of vision becoming conscious of the workings of state power, becoming aware of personal routes to collective consciousness, and becoming empowered to do social justice leadership. Baker understood that as social justice leadership praxis, the "process of becoming" was a persistent and protracted procedure of discourse, debate, consensus, reflection, and struggle. She recognized that the goal of organizing for social justice "was not a single 'end' but rather an ongoing 'means,' that is, a process" (Ransby, 2003, p. 1).

Mary Parker Follett was a late nineteenth-century social activist turned twentieth-century management theorist, and a contemporary of Ella Baker's. She provides a good conceptual frame for understanding radical listening at the point of entry into partnerships (Follett, 1924). Organizers, community development workers, and researchers, whose entry into vulnerable communities can immediately signal hierarchical power relations, especially need to engage in a kind of radical listening that incorporates an intention to engage in coaction. Follett's thesis, similar to Baker's, was based on the recognition of the inevitability of power, a critique of coercive (hierarchical) power, and a call for coactive power fueled by a belief in human capacity. Follett (1924) wrote:

> Genuine power can only be grown, it will slip from every arbitrary hand that grasps it; for genuine power is not coercive control, but coactive control. Coercive power is the curse of the universe; coactive power, *the enrichment and advancement of every human soul.*
>
> *We need a technique of human relations based on the preservation of the integrity of the individual* [emphasis added]. (p. xiii)

In Follett's study of human relations, to be coactive was to stay grounded in concrete daily happenings. Like Baker, Follett understood the imperatives to engage the intractable problems of the time, which persisted, under the weight of "power passing to priests or king or barons, to council or soviet" (p. xii). Yet she called for a coactive approach in organization and innovation that moved beyond old concepts such as compromise and adjustment, or capitalism versus trade unionism. These needed to be replaced with new ideas that would allow us to "seek a way by which desires may interweave, that we seek a method by which the full integrity of the individual shall be one with social progress, that we try to make our daily experience yield for us larger and ever larger spiritual values. . . . We do not want capitalism to 'adjust' itself to trade unionism; we want something better than either of these. We want the plus values of the conflict. This is still adjustment, if you will, but with a more comprehensive meaning than of old" (p. xiv). Follett's concept of coactive process explains theoretically a crucial aspect of radical listening.[5]

Radical listening begins with *perspective taking*, which is one tool for learning empathetic listening. I was in graduate school in my early twenties when I first learned and taught Rogers's theory of empathetic listening (Rogers & Farson, 1957). Reflecting, paraphrasing, and negotiating meaning are communicative tools for helping you stay focused on the other person and their intended meaning before making your own case in an argument. In the 1980s as a graduate teaching assistant in the Department of Speech Communication (now Communication Studies) at California State University, Long Beach, I had full responsibility for teaching courses in public speaking and group communication. I remember what a profound experience it was to watch students doing a simple exercise that required them to take another person's perspective in an argument where there was deep disagreement and then being utterly transformed by the experience. This transformation didn't happen for all students, but for the ones who did experience it, there was a profound moment when they recognized with elegant clarity that seeing another person's view *from that person's perspective* (using another person's words can be as transformative as "walking in that person's shoes") was necessary for being human and having a democracy.

In preparing to enter communities to do social justice work, perspective taking requires that we immerse ourselves in contexts and situations that condition us for empathy. Empathy can be especially challenging for student-service learners, researchers, and practitioners whose ethnic backgrounds and class statuses contrast starkly with those of the people they intend to engage in communities (Camacho, 2004). A tenacious commitment to developing a critical consciousness about the workings of structural power and the capacity for empathy have to be in place when preparing to enter into organization-community partnerships.

A third practice for entering communities is networking for social justice knowledge. This is an important relational practice for decolonizing understandings of power/knowledge relationships, especially at the beginning of social justice leadership work. Who has expertise? What expertise do scholars bring that may meet a community need? Who are the bridge leaders and organic intellectuals "in the know" about how power is already operating in a community? When I write grants to support social justice leadership work, they always include a hefty food budget, because I know that much of our time will be spent in gatherings to create and sustain our work as we make new connections and strengthen existing ones. As Block reminds us, community-building leadership is, centrally, about convening: people gather to create experiences, to connect, and to value that connectedness as human beings (2008, p. 85). Convening spaces of fellowship in which community experts and academic as well as other sources of expertise can connect is vital to orienting a collective toward its work.

Networking spaces for social justice knowledge may be informal, emergent, or formal. Across these forms, the arts and humanities are important for advancing the decolonizing of knowledge, primarily because they can destabilize and transform knowledge hierarchies (Barinaga & Parker, 2013). Indigenous practices, such as circles, dance parties, and other events, are important examples of this. One of my current graduate students, for example, is writing her dissertation on the important work of hip-hop DJs in creating spaces of healing in antiracist work. National and regional gatherings, such as the SNCC anniversary events, Gathering for Justice, and Yes! Jams, provide wonderful spaces to seed social justice projects. Other gatherings are more formal, such as conferences or even special community councils, which have the purpose of supporting the power and impact of community voices in organization-university initiatives.

Networking for social justice that is *not* attuned to community power risks being co-opted by organizations to advance neoliberal aims. This has occurred, for example, in "community visioning" exercises in cities, where convening a gathering of community groups vulnerable to precarious housing situations leads to nothing more than a "checked box" and a superficial requirement fulfilled on a city's agenda for unfettered gentrification and the displacement of those groups (Gallent, 2014). Even when such a nefarious intent is absent, social justice networking that isn't attuned to the workings of hierarchical power can inadvertently silence community voices in partnerships.

Each of these three practices—critical self-reflexivity, radical listening, and networking for social justice knowledge—conforms to and advances the first commitment in Ella Baker's catalytic leadership approach: that people under the heels of oppression have to be in the leadership when it comes to getting the heels off their necks. The following two vignettes illustrate these critical practices.

HOLDING STORIES: BETWEEN HORROR AND HOPE

In 2003, I first began to contemplate an engaged research project working alongside African American teen girls in vulnerable communities. Still on the tenure track, and while finishing a book about Black women corporate leaders (Parker, 2004), I began spending time with some of the mothers and their daughters from the Regal Gardens and University Heights public housing neighborhoods in activities organized through my church. My training in qualitative methods prompted me to build on my initial immersion in the neighborhoods with a broader and more focused investigation to hear Black girls and women speak about their lives. In 2004, I conducted a series of interviews with girls and young women in Durham and Raleigh who could bear witness to the everyday contexts of young Black women's lives (Parker, 2005, 2006). These interviews revealed a glimpse of the persistent precarity that pervades Black life in the US economy. Guinier and Torres (2009) refer to this condition as the miner's canary. The state of Black lives is an indicator that the whole economic structure is about to fail.

Two young women's stories in particular sensitized me, not only to the precariousness of Black girls' lives *across* class statuses, but also to communities as spaces of contradictions, ambiguities, and heterogeneity that contain a multiplicity of stories. No one story can be privileged to define the numerous routes to collective consciousness and social justice practice. But stories can shine a light on particular angles, such as the need to be accountable witnesses in communities that experience the horrors of poverty, sexual violence, and racism (Fosl, 2008).

Carrie Jefferson and Daisha Sawyer were two students at Shaw University whom I interviewed in 2006 as part of my preparation for starting the work with Black girls learning social justice activism.[6] As a composite, Carrie's and Daisha's lives were similar to that of the title character Precious in the novel *Push* (Sapphire, 1996) and the subsequent movie adaptation, *Precious* (Daniels et al., 2009). Carrie's middle-class status, she said, "was the lie I had to uphold when I went to the upper-class high school I attended. Eventually we were living in the park behind the school, after our family was evicted from our home. This was the 'middle-class lifestyle' where my stepfather molested me, and an uncle raped me."

Daisha told me her parents were "both on drugs. My brothers were drug dealers, and my sister had two children by two different fathers while she was still a teenager. We were always moving around to find shelter, when I finally left home at 16. Eventually, I ended up in a shelter in Dallas where I saw a woman get raped and killed in the bed next to me."

Eventually, both Carrie and Daisha found their way to Shaw University, the historically Black university (HBCU) in Raleigh, North Carolina, that is Ella Baker's alma mater. Both Carrie and Daisha are now thriving; at the time of the interview, they had both shared their stories publicly as part of an initiative to engage their peers in movements for social justice.

When Carrie and Daisha shared their stories with me, they made me question whether I was prepared to enter into a relational space, working alongside people in communities. Hearing these young women's stories made me question whether and how I should hear others' stories. How would I hold them? How should, could, or would they matter to an academic scholar-activist? Ta-Nehisi Coates, a highly acclaimed journalist, intellectual leader, and (at the time) senior editor at the *Atlantic*, described his foray into storytelling in his groundbreaking piece "The Case for Reparations." He was excited about how easy and energizing it was to go and ask someone to tell a story: that person tells you, and then you write about it. He said something like, "That's it? You'll pay me for this?" (Coates, 2014). I had the opposite reaction as I entered into this work of being a conduit of people's stories. What gives me the right? And to what ends? Telling stories is a powerful tool for the structural analysis of politics, history, race, and culture, as Coates has illustrated. However, I understood, following Michelle Fine, that power and method are all tied up together. Depending on how they are deployed, stories can be a catalyst for change. Or they can be used unwittingly to reinforce neoliberal projects supporting discourses of free market individualism, efficiency, and victim blaming (Fine, 1994).

Over time I came to understand that what was embedded in Carrie's and Daisha's stories were the seeds for a deeper structural analysis of the root causes of the violence that pervaded these young women's early lives. These kinds of stories are left out of the mandates to "just work harder—follow the rules-policies-procedures-pronouncements-findings-results-studies-who's-in-who-survives-who-deserves-who-made-it-who-can-make-it-who-should-make-it—Why didn't you get here at 10:00? Just do what it takes, dammit!" There is no readily accessible mechanism in the public consciousness (media, schools, institutions) to trace these young women's stories through the very historical structures of White supremacy, racism, and violence against Black bodies that helped produce the interpersonal and systemic violence. That is the analysis that must be brought to the fore (as Coates has done in his role as cultural critic).

But at the moment they shared their stories, I was thinking that on one level, I had no right to receive those stories. Yes, I had approval from the institutional review board to interview them using a protocol that the women themselves had seen and agreed to follow. They knew that I would write up their stories as part of my research on Black girls and young women doing activism. But on another level, I was thinking, "What am I doing? What should I be doing? How can I just listen to those stories as if that's the most normal thing in the world to do? *Am I* just like all the other people Carrie mentioned when she told me, 'You can't depend on people to do anything for you. Everyone just wants what they want from you?'"

Hearing these young women's personal testimonies alerted me to the need to develop a capacity for "holding stories" in a way that moves with people toward action and social justice and away from a debilitating stasis that is often tied to the frustration of structural failures. For scholar-activists working with people in some of the most precarious life situations, "holding stories" means encountering the sheer emotional weight of another person's suffering but also being able to listen for and support the potential for resilience. When I asked Daisha and Carrie about how they had survived—and what they thought was meant by "thriving," for example—they both pointed to opportunities they had had to see their own internal qualities, which they had relied on to bring them through the darkest times. At the same time, they called in the need for a societal structure that recognizes the gaps in the social fabric, which they almost slipped through.[7]

Scholar-activists are called to navigate the spaces between "horror and hope" alongside people working to survive multiple systems of oppression.

In my years of working alongside the young women and their allies at Regal Gardens and University Heights, I encountered stories—their own or those of someone close to them—that were similar to Carrie's and Daisha's. I have learned two lessons about the capacity for navigating the spaces between horror and hope.

First, it calls for a level of critical self-reflexivity that begins with questioning our own positionality. That involves, most crucially, recognizing that we are not "saviors" but rather part of a broader complex of human capital being engaged to intervene in a particular context of power relations. It requires a process of constant questioning of our own claims and motives, with an intention to engage in radical listening and mutual learning (Schwarz, 2013). Scholar-activists with such an intention might pursue the following line of questioning, as my students and I attempted to do when we began the collaboration with girls and their families in Regal Gardens and University Heights: What are we called to create together? What is needed in this moment to advance the cause of social justice? What expertise do I or the organization I represent bring to the partnership? How do community members calling for social justice understand that expertise? How might I be helping or hindering the process? The challenge comes not in formulating the questions but in learning to listen for and engage with the responses. As Ella Baker cautioned, we must be attuned to the people living under the heels of oppression to guide the process. As shown in this case study, sometimes the institutional mindsets that scholar-activists bring with us when we enter communities can block the capacity for staying attuned to the expertise of people in communities.

Second, radical listening—listening to silences and hearing the need, as Baker taught, underscored by Follett (1924), to "nourish the individual"—beckons us to slow our pace as we enter communities and note the places where healing from trauma, including our own, is being called in. Carrie's and Daisha's stories helped me understand that holding stories in organization-community collaborations is a deeply relational process that requires development over time. Communities structured for healing and built on the assets of those living there have long understood this (Ginwright, 2010).

I rejected the notion, for example, of starting a project that involved a one-off process of collecting stories to advance a particular theme. Having been recently tenured, knowing that I was at a university that supported engaged research, and working with people in a neighborhood very near my university all helped me make that commitment to a long-term partnership. However, not every scholar-activist has those advantages. This is especially true for graduate students in the early stages of their dissertation research projects. However, if researchers are committed to the first foundational commitment to catalytic social justice leadership—that the community members and their needs should decide the direction of organization-community collaborations—then dissertation projects must be contingent on the capacity to serve as one intervention on a longer horizon. Whether the graduate student continues as part of the longer partnership, then, becomes less important than an understanding of how that student, and their work, fits into the broader complex of human capital being engaged to intervene in a particular context of power relations.

REMAKING THE RULES

After the 2006 interviews, I continued to contemplate starting a community-based partnership with Black girls and their allies, now even more sure of my desire to develop a decolonizing research praxis. Such a praxis would support a commitment to participatory research: my students and I would work with people in vulnerable communities through a continuous process of dialogic practice and reflection that supported girls' development as leaders. I intended for us to do a praxis that would allow us to analyze our own complicity with oppression and demand that we remain accountable to all involved in the research, from the naming of the project and its purposes to the research products that emerged from it (Baker, 2005). Decolonizing research challenges the institution of academic research. It is a "purposeful agenda for transforming . . . the deep underlying structures and taken-for-granted ways of organizing, conducting, and disseminating research and knowledge" (Smith, 2005, p. 88). Decolonizing research necessitates remaking the rules in some instances.

The project launched in May 2007, and the Ella Baker Women's Center was established in a repurposed unit in Regal Gardens. It was situated "down the hill" from University Heights, which was positioned "up top," in the parlance of neighborhood residents. However, even before the project launched, the girls and their allies living in Regal Gardens and University Heights revealed themselves to be organizers. This was the first indication that my students and I were the ones being organized and researched, which was essential to the emerging decolonizing praxis.

I had first been introduced to some of the mothers and their young daughters in Regal Gardens and University Heights in 2003—four years before the founding of the center—through my work as a leader in the Women's Missionary Society at St. Paul African Methodist Episcopal (AME) Church in Chapel Hill.[8] Each spring I helped organize a "mother-daughter" picnic, at which residents and women from the church would gather in a sunny banquet room nearby to share box lunches and reflect on the wisdom of our mothers. Later, I began spending time in the neighborhood, volunteering in the after-school program for middle-school students and generally getting to know the families, mostly by sitting on the stoop with some of the women as their children played nearby.

Although I don't think I realized it at the time, it was during this period that I began to hone my capacity for networking for social justice knowledge. Like Baker, I was learning to listen for "hidden transcripts" that held resonances of state surveillance, resistance, and ways to do things better (J.C. Scott, 1990). Something in my own experience readily heard and absorbed these resonances. Perhaps it was the echoes of similar conversations from my childhood in rural Arkansas; perhaps because I'd been steeped in the literature of Black women's legacies of critical resistance, which was informing and contextualizing the book I was finishing about leadership traditions in the life stories of African American women corporate executives (Parker, 2004). Whatever the reason, I was drawn to linger in the neighborhood after my tutoring duties were finished, and this shaped the start of our work together. We were beginning to see each other as experts on our own terms, from our different angles of vision. The organizing had begun before any of us realized it was happening.

As some of the moms in the neighborhood learned that I was thinking about developing a leadership program for high school girls, they encouraged me to start the program right in their neighborhood instead of in another part of the region, the site I had been considering. "You should do your program in *our* neighborhood, Ms. Pat! We don't have anything for the older kids," Ms. Lynetta, Tania's mom, told me. Ms. Dorita, Vanessa's mom, nodded her head in agreement. Another mom, Ms. Naomi, whose two teen boys and six-year-old daughter, Moni, were regular participants in the programs at the Family Resource Center, told me, "You're the first Black professor I know of from the university that's come over here to do research. It's mostly the White ones."[9]

Those conversations eventually led to the planning and launch of the Still Lifting, Still Climbing (SLSC) Leadership Program for Black teen girls at Regal Gardens and University Heights in the summer of 2007. It became the first project of the budding collective described in the introduction that involved allies, community experts, and the teen girls, some introduced earlier in this chapter; myself; two student interns; a university-funded consultant with expertise in youth organizing; one of the moms, Ms. Vergie, who was already serving in an activist role; and Ms. Delores Bailey, who had been doing transformative work in the community for almost a decade.

This was to be a summer program following Baker's philosophy that "the people living under the heels of oppression should be the ones leading." The moms in the neighborhood had identified an area of need, and some of the teen girls I had met seemed excited about starting something just for them. I wanted to make sure that I stayed focus on that need, supporting the seeds of resistance that seemed to be present. I believed that Baker was the practical embodiment of African American women's tradition of leadership-as-resistance, and her philosophy of community organizing was one that I wanted to learn by doing.

.   .   .   .   .

The first time I met Jamilla she was walking home from town with her mother, Ms. Sheritha, and her two twin brothers, LaDon and LaMon. It was early spring 2007, just a few weeks before the launch of the program that would become the flagship initiative of the Ella Baker Women's Center. Jamilla was eleven and not yet at the established thirteen-year-old threshold for participation in what would become the first S3! girls' leadership cohort. Her twin brothers were around age four at the time of our encounter on the sidewalk. I had not seen Jamilla in attendance at any of the programs for middle-school kids at the center, nor had she and her mother, Ms. Sheritha, participated in any of the mother-daughter picnics. However, I had met Ms. Sheritha a few times when she had come to pick up her boys, who were attending a program for preschoolers at the Family Resource Center, and I had also seen her in the University Heights neighborhood. She had mentioned several times that she wanted to make sure Jamilla was involved in the program. The invitations had been distributed, and Jamilla was not among those who had received one. As I approached in my car the place where they were walking, I stopped, and they all came up to the passenger-side window.

"Ms. Pat, this is Jamilla," Ms. Sheritha said proudly.

"Hi," Jamilla said.

I said hello back, with a big smile.

Ms. Sheritha said, "Ms. Pat! I want Jamilla to be in the group!"

I said something like, "Well the group is just for high school girls right now and the starting age is thirteen [ninth grade]." But in my heart, I was thinking that that was wrong.

In 1960, Ella Baker challenged the gathering of civil rights leaders at Shaw University to "be radical" in following the example of the young people who had been leading sit-in movements across the country. She saw in their actions the kind of courage to directly challenge the status quo through nonviolent protest at the point of power: the unjust laws of racial segregation. Ms. Baker advocated "remaking the rules" of tradition that would have brought the young activists into the fold of the larger, less agile organizations, such as the Southern Christian Leadership Coalition headed by Dr. King. Instead, she insisted that young people should have their own organization to continue the trajectory of their activism. Consequently, SNCC was formed, and Ella Baker became its primary mentor.

The lessons from Baker's example that informed my entry into University Heights and Regal Gardens were to ask radical questions and to resist the logics of tradition. For example, I was following the typical way that research starts in community projects: find a site, create research questions, and secure funding. That had all been written up in my application to the university's institutional review board. To ask radical questions and resist tradition involves questioning the status quo, as Baker had.

In retrospect, my response to Ms. Sheritha about her eleven-year-old daughter's participation was very telling. It revealed the ambivalence I had in those early days about my relationship to the people in the neighborhood. I saw myself on some levels as an insider, but at the same time I was someone whom residents saw as the controller of resources.

My response also revealed how much I had to learn about putting into practice Baker's philosophy of community organizing. On the one hand, I knew that the residents wanted a formal youth program: a structured program for older kids to have something to be involved in after school. Most of the programs offered in the neighborhood were for the younger kids in kindergarten and middle school. I also thought I needed to show parents, and the administrators of the grant that was funding the work, that there were "standards" guiding the SLSC summer program (i.e., age requirements and other stipulations).

On the other hand, I knew that my most important expertise was my capacity to meet people where they are, as Baker did; to be in it for the long haul; and to work in solidarity with people who were trying to change the narratives circulating around and through their neighborhoods. That understanding was foundational to Baker's philosophy of organizing. This was, above all, community work *with* people in a neighborhood that is already vulnerable because of random policies enforced at will without community input, and by other actions of decision makers at a distance.[10] Bob Moses is perhaps the person who worked most closely with Ella Baker; as of this writing, he continues to organize "in the spirit of Ella." He has reinforced this aspect of Baker's organizing philosophy:

> In contrast to the university-based researcher, the organizer working in the tradition of Ella gradually becomes recognized by community members as having a commitment to their overall well-being. The organizer immerses him- or herself in the life of the community, learning its strengths, resources, concerns, and ways of conducting business. The organizer does not have a comprehensive, detailed plan for remedying a perceived problem, but takes an "evolutionary" view of his or her own role in the construction of the solution. He or she understands that the community's everyday concerns can be transformed into broader political questions of general import. The form they will take is not always known in advance. (Moses et al., 1989, p. 439)

Perhaps sensing the "evolutionary" view I was beginning to develop, I later realized that Ms. Sheritha was asking a question that was cluing me in to the most important aspect of my presence in the neighborhood. She was letting me know that she wanted her daughter to be a part of something important in the community. She was saying, "My daughter is here. My daughter is a leader. You of all people should see that, 'Ms. Black Lady Organizer!'" But at the time, I missed that message on a very fundamental level. True, there were issues of funding and resources, but also in that moment, the tug of a "repeatable project" with stipulations, criteria, and boundaries was winning out over my desire to be in community *with* Ms. Sheritha and her family.

Jamilla did participate in the group that year, and in the years that followed, circling in and out of participation in the activities the youth organized, always engaging on her own terms.[11] I realize now that in our encounter on the sidewalk that day, she and Ms. Sheritha had taught me an important lesson about the need to sometimes remake the rules in university-organization partnerships.

Indeed, that lesson was first foregrounded when Vanessa's and Tania's moms asked me to do the girls' leadership project in *their* neighborhood. Their requests caused me to question my original intention to choose a site for my research based on statistics and other data that seemed to indicate areas with the most vulnerability. Vanessa's and Tania's moms were calling my attention to what was under the radar of published statistics. In places such as a college town with extreme income gaps, the effects of state violence are often felt more acutely. Bob Moses counseled that we should throw down our bucket where we were (Moses et al., 1989). I stayed in the neighborhood that had called me in to do the work of social justice.

As the preceding vignette illustrates, critically engaged social justice activism requires that "we make the road by walking," in Horton and Freire's (1990) terms. Especially in the case of university-community engagement, that often means having to rethink our purposes for starting projects in the first place and remaking the neoliberal purposes that often mask the intentions of the state, foundations, and corporations to control and surveil. We need to immerse ourselves in community networks *prior* to entering into community-based partnerships. This allows us to listen for the silences and stay attuned to historical contexts of settler colonialism that reveal what is possible in the present.

.   .   .   .   .

Rewriting the rules is necessary because of the often entrenched mindsets of academics and nonprofits in the neoliberal state. Kwon (2013) theorized this entrenchment as "affirmative governmentality." Kwon investigated the political conditions that both enable and limit youth of color from achieving meaningful change given the entrenchment of nonprofits in the logics of the neoliberal state. These logics become evident, for example, in the proliferation of after-school and community-based programs mobilized to prevent potentially "at-risk" youth from turning to "juvenile delinquency" and crime, with interventions that seek to mold young people to become self-empowered and responsible citizens. Kwon drew on several years of ethnographic research with an Oakland-based, pan-ethnic youth organization that promotes grassroots activism among its second-generation Asian and Pacific Islander members (ages fourteen to eighteen). While analyzing the contradictions of the youth-organizing movement, Kwon documented the genuine contributions to social change made by the young people with whom she worked in an era of increased youth criminalization and anti-immigrant legislation.

Presumably the youth in Kwon's study made genuine contributions to social change despite the "subalterning" effects of neoliberal youth-organizing strategies or reading these youth as isolated and silenced mutes (Spivak, 1988). Kwon's study raises important questions: How do we create spaces for "genuine contributions to social change"? What nuances distinguish spaces that perpetuate governmentality and those that create the potential for individual revolutionary acts (e.g., so that people see their own actions as connected to larger structural oppressions) and a critical collective consciousness to emerge? In other words, how does the radical thinker avoid getting co-opted? Our collective's direct attempt at doing that began with the Dumpster Project, discussed in the next chapter. At the time we saw it as a failure, but it was later understood as the start of the catalytic leadership process.

This chapter has responded to the question, *How should people from outside communities—students, faculty, volunteers, administrators—be prepared emotionally, intellectually, and practically to take into account complexities that situate organizational-community collaborations?* The vignettes provide some takeaways that I hope you will find helpful in your work. I want to underscore the need for direct training to learn antiracist theories and participatory research—through undergraduate and graduate school courses, community certification programs, and other sources. Educational opportunities abound for in-depth learning through racial equity initiatives and participatory research certificate programs. However, I have learned that the most productive training comes with the opportunity to actually do the work of testing theories in practice, creating praxis in a specific context. Some certificate programs provide that kind of immersion (Parker et al., 2018). On the other hand, racial equity training, which has become a robust industry in education, universities, and nongovernmental organizations (NGOs), can in some ways have the opposite impact. There is a danger that these types of trainings become one-off, pro forma events whose participants never directly test their developing critical consciousness about race and power (the underlying focus of racial equity training) (Schillinger, 2017). What is required is a praxis—the application of theory plus action plus critical self-reflection—in a continuous feedback loop to transform individuals, systems, and society (Argyris & Schön, 1996; Weick, 1995). I have come to understand the building of a race-critical praxis as an ongoing learning process.

Before entering the partnership with the girls and their allies in Regal Gardens and University Heights, I had been researching and writing about critical race and organizational communication for several years (Parker, 1996, 2003a, 2003b, 2004). In addition, in the weeks leading up to the formation of the partnership, I was intentional about training my students and other adult allies in Baker's grassroots organizing principle of believing in the power of people in communities to define their own problems and participate in social justice actions for change. However, as we began the youth engagement work that the residents at University Heights and Regal Gardens had invited us to do, there were lessons to learn about how our positioning within the formal organization of the university would deeply impact relationships across the lines of difference in our partnership, especially those of race, gender, class, and generation.

Our budding collective's work was situated within the paradoxical space of needing and gaining institutional support that at the same time became an almost immediate barrier to establishment of the trust required for productive and accountable collaborations. As well-intentioned and semiprepared as I might have thought I was when my students and I entered into the partnership with the girls and their allies in Regal Gardens and University Heights, I did not fully anticipate how much that paradoxical context would impact our work. The next chapter explains what happened and how we responded.

3 "Think in Radical Terms"

CREATING PARTICIPATIVE SPACES
FOR SOCIAL JUSTICE ORGANIZING

In the summer of 2007, the Ella Baker Women's Center's collective began its youth engagement work with the residents at University Heights and Regal Gardens. In a core partnership with youth and adult allies in the collective, we launched our first social justice leadership projects, the Dumpster Project in fall 2007 and the CommUNITY Festival in fall 2008. The lessons learned through the Dumpster Project, which we saw at first as a setback, catalyzed our collective to become a *community-driven* social justice organizing process thereafter.

This chapter engages with two central questions. First, what motivates individual routes to social justice leadership given the conditions of extreme capitalism? The encounter with Jamilla's mother on the sidewalk, described in the previous chapter, hinted at the search for positive routes to the future that parents typically hope to find for their children. At the same time, I was also aware that in vulnerable communities those routes often are embedded within the context of surveillance and control mechanisms in extreme capitalist systems meant to create a steady supply of pliable, disposable labor (Deetz, 1992; Foucault, 1977; Meade, 2017).

The potential for agency depends in part on "what people think might be possible, thinkable, desirable, or necessary in a particular place."[1] There are multiple routes to activism within a context in which history has taught that "keeping your head down" is a proven ideology for survival in a culture not intended to ensure that survival (Lorde, 1995). Ella Baker taught that the motivation to lead from such contexts emerges in the terms of people in that context. It emerges when they are participating in "free spaces" where common sense about survival can be transformed into a liberating power for social justice. The story of the Dumpster Project proved that our collective had not quite accomplished our learning in that area.

The second question that guided our work, and that guides this chapter, is what would truly participative spaces look like, in which productive knowledge could emerge from all angles of vision and from people at various stages of becoming socially conscious? When differently positioned and resourced allies in universities (or other organizations) collaborate with people in vulnerable communities, the capacity to create "free spaces" for individual routes to collective consciousness can be challenging because of hierarchical power. In a community-based partnership with inherent hierarchical differences—in our case, institutional, generational, and racialized—we had to learn how crucial it was to be intentional about Ella Baker's second commitment to catalyzing social justice leadership, which states that when decisions put lives at stake, we should use tenaciously participative decision-making structures that tilt toward the least powerful in that arrangement. Thinking in those radical terms meant that our collective needed to learn hard lessons about how to implement practices that nurture girls' voices in a productive dialectical process with their allies' voices. How our collective was able to do that is recounted later in this chapter in the story of our collective's first youth-led and community-driven project—the CommUNITY Festival—after the false starts we experienced with the Dumpster Project.

Lessons from both the Dumpster Project and the CommUNITY Festival illustrate the communication practices applied through a commitment to create participatory structures in which social justice leadership can emerge and be strengthened (see table 3). The description of each project is followed by a primer for applying three participatory communication practices: radical listening to create free spaces, critical dialogic group structure and process, and participative decision-making that tilts toward the least powerful.

Table 3   Creating Participative Spaces for Social Justice Organizing
         Commitment, Problem, and Communication Practices

Commitment	Problem	Communication Practices
Group-centered leadership: "Think in radical terms." (Baker, 1969/1999)	**Participation:** problems of hierarchical difference that thwart the strategic use of different kinds of power/knowledge resources	• Radical listening for creating "free spaces": listening for context; listening for silences; listening for multiple angles of vision • Critical dialogic group structure and processes: group facilitation capacities for everyone; discussions about different forms of expertise; mutual learning structures that support trial and error; circle processes that encourage dialogue; rotating leadership roles • Participative decision-making: tilted toward the least powerful when there are threats to humanity

THE DUMPSTER PROJECT: THE ELLA BAKER WOMEN'S CENTER COLLECTIVE BEGINS

In June 2007, the summer of the official start of the center's flagship leadership project, seven girls from the neighborhood began a series of workshops. My students and I, along with adult allies from the community, spent the weeks before the kickoff event designing summer workshops. These were based on my preliminary research on Ella Baker's philosophy. They were also informed by my research on models of youth-adult partnerships for intergenerational leadership. Elayne Dorsey, a Kellogg Foundation fellow I had met through community networking, had introduced me to the groundbreaking work of the Kellogg Leadership for Community Change (KLCC) program, which was designed to learn from grassroots social justice change organizations across the United States (Ospina & Foldy, 2010). Elayne was also a consultant with the Innovation Center for

Community and Youth Development, and I had contracted to work with her to help get our youth-adult partnership collective started. Both KLCC and the Innovation Center had tool kits and curriculum guides with activities for arts activism, youth organizing, and youth participatory research. Those resources, along with my own research on Ella Baker and other sources on bridge leadership, informed the development of the Ella Baker Women's Center's initial curriculum for a seven-week program designed to prepare the girls to colead a project with adult allies (see appendix 1).

The girls each received a personal invitation to the kickoff event, along with a colorful flyer that heralded the program's intention to create a safe space for them to express themselves as leaders in their communities. "Young Women of Color Speak!!!" was emblazoned across the top of the flyer, and there was graphic art depicting young women speaking into a microphone, playing music, and dancing. To be sure, the first gathering was an emergent process meant for discovery. We were all experimenting. We wondered what would happen if we invited girls to a special luncheon—girls who, I later learned, had lived through histories similar to what the students at Shaw University had shared with me. What would happen if we told them that we had heard them when they said that they wanted a space for their voices to be heard? What if we told them that they were special and that their parents had told us so, that they had special gifts and capacities for a project we wanted to launch together with them? That was the language on the invitation. It was meant as an intervention into the discourses and stories that circulate through Black girls' lives. Narratives about belonging and worth permeate the places and spaces where their agency is enacted at home, in school, on the streets, and around the neighborhood. The girls are steeped in narratives that may alternatively reinforce or reject their self-worth. In some spaces around College Town, including at the university, they might be seen as "space invaders," raced and gendered bodies out of place in spaces of White privilege (Puwar, 2004). The invitation was meant to signal to the girls that we intended to be accountable to them.

The girls were experimenting, too. They came to the gathering based on an invitation, their parents' hope for the project, and a tentative trust in adult activists from inside and outside of the community who called them in.

It was a hot, humid afternoon on the day of the gathering, typical for that time of year in North Carolina. Seven teenage girls were seated around an executive conference room table at the EmPOWERment Center on Geer Street, alongside six adult allies in their twenties, thirties, and forties. Box lunches lined the counter at the back of the room, along with brightly colored gift bags that matched the explosion of color that the girls wore: tops in bright magenta, turquois, red, and one with "GIRLS" written in pink across the front. This was the kickoff for the Still Lifting, Still Climbing summer leadership project with girls and their allies that would launch the flagship program, which would come to be called Striving Sisters Speak! (S3!). There was a feeling of excitement in the room—an expectation that something was going to happen just because of the people who had gathered there.

In the room were two students from the university, Joaquín and Elisa, both trained in participatory action research methods. During this time, I was the faculty research mentor to Elisa and Joaquín, who were completing a ten-week research apprenticeship (MURAP, described in the introduction), funded by a national foundation. Joaquín was finishing up his undergraduate studies at Eugene Lang College in New York (the New School), and Elisa was in her senior year at Humboldt State University in California. Both Joaquín and Elisa had been immersed in activism in their respective communities. Joaquín, a queer Latinx activist from Chicago, had been working with youth in Brooklyn and had recently helped initiate a gang intervention group comprised of youth activists in a high school in the Bushwick (Brooklyn) community. Elisa, a daughter of first-generation Mexican immigrants, had been doing feminist activism work with women of color in California and participating in Acción Zapatista, a collective committed to theorizing and practicing Zapatismo, a movement that emphasizes the relationships among action, dignity, and resistance to neoliberalism locally.[2]

At the table also was Ms. Vergie, the already engaged activist who lived in the girls' neighborhood. Ms. Vergie had lived in the neighborhood for seven years and was the mother of six-year-old Michael. She is *that* Black woman—the one who notices Black girls' beginning to see themselves in their world, carrying themselves in a particular way, learning, as Ms. Vergie says, to be "*young ladies.*" However, the way Ms. Vergie engages the girls in her neighborhood, and what she is teaching them about growing up as a Black girl, is not about the politics of respectability (White, 2010).

She is a bridge leader. She is teaching about survival and learning in a world that is at times predatory and unjust.

At that gathering and in the years that followed, Ms. Vergie was a constant guide for my students and me as she bridged the organizational-community divides that were an almost immediate barrier to our work. She had ties to the historically Black community in College Town, but she had not grown up there. Yet she was connected to other bridge leaders who had deep roots in the neighborhood and to whom she connected us.

Ms. Vergie was aware of the "goings-on" in the community and had an analysis of how power created "limit situations" for people trying to realize their capacity through civic agency. On more than one occasion, she reminded me that people in the community want to advocate for their children just like any other parents. But "when you're working two jobs or being forced to work a night shift because of your job status," it's tough to attend PTA meetings or help with homework.[3] Through her involvement with the youth in the community and as a town appointee on governance boards, she saw her role as both a grassroots leader and a more formal civic leader. She became a key ally in our group as we worked to discover and define catalyzing questions to intervene in social change problems identified by neighborhood residents.

Delores Bailey from EmPOWERment was also in the room. Delores is a community bridge leader who is committed to doing social justice work in the communities in which she was raised. As executive director of EmPOWERment, Delores had continued the work begun in 1996 by two students from the UNC School of Social Work, Myles Presler and Termain Kyles, who had heard directly from residents about some of their challenges. Those issues included high housing costs, low-quality housing, political and economic disempowerment, and low household incomes. These are persistent local manifestations of systemic issues and structural inequalities in the United States. Starting in 2002, Delores had worked alongside predominantly Black residents in some of the most economically depressed areas of the region to achieve their goals of homeownership or other forms of safe and stable housing, while also organizing with them to transform the structural conditions that were impacting them. Like many of the Black community bridge leaders who came before her, she has worked behind the scenes. In a recent attempt to reverse that trend, the local United Way organization selected Delores Bailey as one of "10 to Watch," an initiative created to address the racial and cultural disparities between the leaders of nonprofit organizations and the communities they serve.

Prior to joining the Ella Baker Women's Center collective, I had come to know Delores Bailey as someone whose heart is with the youth who suffer the weight of living in an elite college town in their Black and Brown bodies and with few economic resources.

Stacey Craig was also in the room. Stacey is representative of the myriad twenty- to thirty-year-old White female scholar-activists who work with youth of color. As a fellow with the AmeriCorps organization, Stacey ran afterschool programs for middle-school children at the neighborhood Family Resource Center.[4] Stacey provided my main entry into the University Heights and Regal Gardens housing communities around 2006, when I started volunteering in the after-school program and getting to know the families there. With a master's degree in social work, Stacey was keenly aware of public housing as a complex site historically for community engagement. She and I often shared deep conversations about how critical race consciousness affected our work at Regal Gardens and University Heights. Importantly, Stacey lived within walking distance of the girls' neighborhood, which deepened her commitment to be in solidarity with the girls and their families.

Later that summer Jennifer Mease, a doctoral student in critical organizational communication studies and my advisee, joined the collective. And in 2009, with in-kind funding through the regional AmeriCorps office, Rachel Valentine joined our collective as a staff member assigned solely to the Ella Baker Women's Center. Rachel was instrumental in working with me and others in the collective to develop our critical pedagogy to apply Baker's philosophies. Like Stacey, Jenn and Rachel were young women who were critically aware of how their Whiteness might affect their work in the community.

In the years that followed, several other young women joined our collective in their capacities as undergraduate student–service learners or summer research interns. However, the contours of our core group of adult allies in the partnership remained the same: myself, the two bridge leaders, two summer research interns, and two to three service learners.

And finally, at the table that first day were seven girls; five were African American girls from University Heights and Regal Gardens and two others were sisters, recently relocated from New York City, who identified as Puerto Rican and lived in a nearby neighborhood.[5] After two weeks these two girls, Selena and Christine, stopped coming. Their father refused to let them return after the younger sister reportedly took a detour on her way home from the center and was not home when expected. Delores Bailey and I met with the parents and offered to transport the girls (even though the center was within a five-minute walk). The girls' father was adamant that having the girls leave the program was the right thing to do, and that was the last I saw of the girls.

The remaining five girls—Vanessa, D'Misha, Yvonne, Jade, and Tina—were later joined by seven other girls from the neighborhood—Tracey, Taliah, Taylor, Chantel (Jade's sister), Tania, Kennedy, and Crystal—who formed the core group that would launch the collective's first two projects. Two additional girls—Tawanna and Shana—joined the following year and became active members until they graduated from high school or moved away from the neighborhood. The girls ranged in age from thirteen to eighteen, and eventually there were activities that paired the older girls with younger girls, like Jamilla, mentioned in the previous chapter, Chanelle and Kiesha, sister and cousin to Yvonne, and Moni, a close cousin to Jade and Chantel.

At the time of this writing, S3! has directly engaged thirty girls affiliated with these two communities and surrounding ones, and a new cohort of ten girls who live in a nearby housing community is taking up the S3! mantle. All forty girls have shaped or are still shaping the story of the Ella Baker Women's Center. However, the initial cohorts will tell the story of what it can mean to be a Black girl activist in the New Jim Crow era. They provide glimpses of a community-university engagement entangled in race, economic precarity, power, and privilege—and even so they reveal what is possible.

. . . . .

Why couldn't they go and say this little boy [Emmett Till] was innocent . . . ? Why'd they let go those two White dudes? Why'd they set them free? . . . Why were they allowed to do that?
—D'Misha, age fourteen, during a workshop at the Ella Baker Women's Center, June 2007

I don't know what I'm going to do, but I'm going to do something . . .
—Rosa Parks, age forty-two, during a workshop at the Highlander Research and Education Center, 1955

Consciousness-raising is (still) a viable project for African American girls who live in a public housing community, as it was for Rosa Parks and her contemporaries. Becoming conscious of that gap between what *is* and what *should be* is a call to action. At the kickoff gathering on that hot June afternoon in 2007, the girls participated in the first of seven workshops we held that summer to get them ready to lead their first social justice project. This first workshop was on the history of youth activism and was intended to initiate a participative space for girls' voices to be centered.

As we all settled in with our box lunches, we began the gathering with an opening circle process that invited all in the room to speak their names. Next, Joaquín led the group through an activity to create our space as a safe space. In this process, youth decided what constituted a safe space and created agreements about it. Almost immediately, between bites of sandwiches and mixed fruit, the girls began to speak as the experts, as only they could be, on aspects of their lives. They talked about places they felt safe and where they knew they were not safe. Vanessa spoke about catcalls on the street from older men as she and her friends walked by. D'Misha talked about the call of gangs she had experienced and what she had learned about how kids can resist them if they have alternatives: someplace to go after school or someone to be with at school. We also talked about relational agreements and how we would share our conversational space. Joaquín captured all of our agreements on a large poster board. They included phrases like "free to make mistakes" and "attack the problem, not the person." We all signed the poster board, signaling our commitment to holding a safe space.

Next, Elisa and Ms. Vergie led a discussion of a slideshow that showed some iconic photographs from the history of activism in US history. Among them was a photo of Emmett Till, which generated a great deal of energy among the girls, who had learned about how the story of Emmett Till's death catalyzed activism in the 1950s amid the racial violence of that time. Two of the girls, Selena and Christine, said that they had never heard the story of Emmett Till. D'Misha also presented the history of what had happened. Slowly, and deliberately, she told the story of Emmett as a teen-ager, about their age, being brutally murdered by two White men in Mississippi. All of us were riveted by D'Misha's account of Emmett's murder.

The telling of the story seemed to spark something in D'Misha. It was during that discussion that she asked the questions quoted at the beginning of this section about why this terrible thing was allowed to happen. Ms. Vergie spoke the following words into the space of that gathering, as some of the girls became aware for the first time of youth activism inspired by the killing of Emmett Till:

> It's not that we as people haven't said anything. It's that everything is not documented. Ok. Everything is not documented. There were people that were lynched and it was not documented. . . . Because it's not like we didn't say anything. It wasn't just like all White people hated Black people. It wasn't like that. If you look at any march, you see a lot of White people up there too. Arm and arm, linked. That's the way we have to look at it and you take it from that stance, and you say, "Well these things, these images that I see up here, now it makes [sense]." You said you don't like the way they did him? That's enough fire in your belly, you say, "You know what? I wanna make a move, I wanna study on this situation, I wanna know why such and such . . ." and you can gather up enough information for you or to pass on to future generations or our group.

The conversation about Emmett Till sparked the girls' interest in youth leading change. It was a natural segue into the next part of the session, during which we watched a short film about the ninth-grade class in a Sacramento high school in the 1970s that advocated for the MLK holiday in California and won over the California State Legislature. Inspired by the youth in the film who led the effort, the girls were excited to get involved in their own communities to lead change.

I repeated a question from the film to guide the discussion: "Do you want to just march for show? Or do you want to bring about real change?"

The girls said they wanted real change.

Then I asked, "What did the group say would be required if they wanted to do real change?"

And they repeated what was in the film: "Get up early; work on Saturdays."

Figure 2. S3! founders and allies at 2007 summer workshops at EmPOWERment, Chapel Hill, NC. Photo by Joaquín Sánchez Jr.

Then I said, "No one is going to ask you to do anything we wouldn't do, nor risk your life. But we are asking for a yearlong commitment to create something together. Are you willing to do that?"

Everyone said, "*Yes.*"

Next it was time to name the group (see figure 2). This involved a lively conversation in which the girls brainstormed names ("Girls Lead" and "Sisters Taking Charge" were high on the list) and finally settled on "Striving Sisters Speak!" Vanessa was adamant that we should have "sisters" in the name because it would signal our strength as women and girls supporting each other. Jade advocated for having some reference to "speaking" in the name, taking a cue from the young activists in the film who spoke at the California State Legislature, and also affirming the girls' desire to "speak their minds" as young women of color. Vanessa then pulled the name together as Striving Sisters Speak! (with three exclamation points at first, but later reduced to just one), and Tania chimed in that it could be S3! for short. Thus, the name S3! was adopted with unanimous acclamation.

After that we went into a brainstorming session, in which the S3! girls talked about what they wanted to see changed in their communities. Vanessa mentioned that it would be good to bring the community together with some sort of party. There was more talk about this, and people were very excited. Joaquín and Elisa were brilliant at affirming the girls' ideas. However, we all agreed that we would hold off on finalizing the focus of the project until we could get more training and build our capacity to do social justice leadership. As the session ended, we worked with the girls to figure out the best schedule for the workshops that would prepare them for their yearlong project. We agreed to meet every Thursday at EmPOWERment and then hold a two-day retreat to reflect on our work and choose our yearlong project.

We ended the kickoff session with a circle process to reflect on the afternoon's work together and have each person speak into the room. Some of the adults spoke first, perhaps because of the logic of how the circle was configured. However, this was a practice that went against the principles of youth-adult partnerships that had informed our initial curriculum. It was one early indication that we were sometimes missing signals related to becoming intentionally youth centered and community driven. Nevertheless, youth and adults alike felt the energy generated by the collective's first gathering for social justice. Elisa captured that energy early in the closing circle, when she spoke of how powerful it was for women of color to speak their minds and put that in historical context.

When it was their turn to speak into the circle, the youths spoke powerfully. Jade and Tania both talked about the importance of creating a safe space for young women to speak freely about what was happening in their lives. Yvonne, who had hardly spoken during the brainstorming sessions, agreed with that assessment. She then shared her opinion that places in College Town that seemed to be designed for youth involvement—including a historic recreational space that was built by and for African American citizens—did not seem to be safe spaces because they did not seem very welcoming.

Ms. Delores was the last to speak into the circle, and she could hardly contain her enthusiasm. She spoke about how the girls had brought up issues that were widespread, not just issues that impacted local, economically vulnerable communities, but issues that youth—especially young women—face everywhere. As a person who is on the inside of College Town politics, she affirmed, "This is a demonstration of power. Youth speaking from their experience is effective, and people notice. If we could bottle it and distribute it everywhere, then that would be a force for change!"

.   .   .   .   .

In the weeks that followed the initial June 2007 kickoff, the members of S3!, along with Joaquín, Elisa, Ms. Vergie, Stacey, Jenn, and I, met for formal social justice advocacy workshops. Vanessa and Jade were clear leaders of the S3! group and were instrumental in inviting three other girls, Tracey, Taliah, and Chantel (Jade's sister), so that we had a group of eight regulars that summer.

However, rarely did all eight girls attend. I recorded in my field notes that attendance seemed to be saying something about the context of the girls' agency—a hidden transcript that was not yet legible to me. One particular week, when I attended a meeting of community service providers that included the staff from preschool, grade-school, and middle-school after-school programs that were currently taking place in the University Heights and Regal Gardens neighborhood, I heard someone say, "It's like pulling teeth to get some of the parents and students to participate in the extracurricular activities at the center." I shared my thinking on the matter, though not yet fully aware of the context. I suggested that perhaps parents and students should be answering the question of participation. Yes, we needed to establish collective accountability. But the meanings of accountability have to take into account the context of people's lived experiences. It was not until years later that I understood what a complex and wholly contingent process this is.

In our case there were certainly intervening events that caused absences: babysitting duty, unscheduled family trips, and the like. However, there was also a testing of boundaries that came up in some of the conversations. The commitment to be accountable to the group, which we had established in the first gathering, was a touchstone for conversations about why some girls were absent on certain days. Most of the time Vanessa or Jade would initiate these conversations in the group, calling in one of the girls they thought had just not bothered to show up.[6] I had also established a good rapport with each of the girls' mothers, and I knew that they were supportive of the girls being part of the program and would provide an extra push as needed. Joaquín, Stacey, Elisa, and I felt we had the flexibility to let the dynamics of attendance play out in the group.[7] This was one effort to follow Ella Baker's way of meeting people where they are on the road to collective consciousness.

The workshops themselves were divided into three segments focused on personal, organizational, and community leadership. The personal and organizational leadership workshops happened over six weeks in June and July, and the community leadership segment occurred at a weekend workshop at the end of August. Each segment had clear objectives and outcomes but with two overarching themes: the meanings of community activism from the perspective of being a teen girl living in a college town and learning leadership, and centering youth-adult partnerships in meaningful collaboration. To keep those themes in view, we maintained flexible structures to create a participative space in which the girls' creative energies could drive weekly conversations about activism and place checks on the adult allies' tendency to dominate the conversations.

The personal leadership workshops helped maintain the momentum from the kickoff, intended to affirm the girls as experts on their own lives and allow the adult allies to share our personal histories. We used art to build a more participative structure that would center the girls' voices. In one activity that generated a great deal of excitement among all participants, we created a series of drawings that depicted "who we are," "who we pretend to be," and "who others think we are." That activity culminated with all of us creating a compact disc cover that featured how we were seeing ourselves in the group. As attendance waxed and waned over the summer, adults often outnumbered youth. However, Elisa had been doing separate *testimonio* workshops with the S3! girls as well as a group of Latina girls from a local Latinx center, which provided an opportunity for a 5:1 youth-to-adult ratio, tilting the structural power more toward the girls.

Around mid-July, after a break for vacations, the group shifted our focus to the organizational leadership workshops. These workshops were intended to help our burgeoning collective begin to see the complex relationship of youth and adults working in partnership for social justice. Each girl was responsible for leading sections of our interactive workshop that explored the obstacles to true youth-adult partnerships. In one activity, "The Spectrum of Attitudes Toward Youth" (Lofquist, 1989), I coached Yvonne as she led the group through an interactive discussion that illustrated the girls' examples of where youth are seen as "objects," "recipients," "resources," or part of "youth and adult partnerships." Most of the girls agreed that prison was the main place where youth were treated as objects and that school could be a place like that as well. I gave a brief lesson on "youth-led" orientations in youth-adult partnerships, the focus of our group. I emphasized that in that scenario, youth should be in the lead, making decisions about the group's direction—especially with our projects—and adults should serve as resources to support them. After some discussion, the group decided that our collective was not quite yet a partnership because the youth had really not made any of the big decisions. However, that was about to change with the community leadership planning retreat.

Elisa's and Joaquín's summer research internships were complete at the end of July, and we decided to have a celebration to mark the occasion. All eight girls were in attendance, signaling their attachment to Joaquín and Elisa's engagement with the group. As part of his research project, Joaquín had prepared a short video, a digital story of our group's work so far. Each of us was given copies of the video. He also promised to return in August to help with the community leadership retreat.

The community leadership portion of the workshops happened a week before classes began at the local high school. We knew that we would include a celebration of the successful completion of our workshop series but would also have a daylong, focused space in which to map out a plan for our yearlong social justice project, led by the girls. We settled on a Friday evening and all-day Saturday structure. As part of their capacity building for organizing events, the girls planned the community gathering on Friday, which included the creation and delivery of invitations to their parents and friends from the neighborhood and potential allies that Ms. Delores and I knew from the larger community.

The Friday evening part of the community leadership retreat was a warm and inviting gathering at the historically African American community center in College Town. The girls had decided on a chili supper for the menu, which was catered by an African woman who owned her own catering business and who, I learned later, had worked in the 1970s as a social worker in Regal Gardens. As with all of our gatherings, we began in a large circle in which one by one, everyone spoke their names, organizational affiliations, and why they were there. The room was filled with close to thirty people: the girls' friends, a few of their parents, some aunts, and some of the younger kids from the neighborhood. There were also community allies who had been hearing about the youth activism focus of the Ella Baker Women's Center from Ms. Delores and me, as well as through Joaquín's and Elisa's community networking during their summer research internships. Each of us—White, Black, and Brown allies who were gathered there to support the youth—spoke into the circle our commitment to social justice and the hope for the future that this youth leadership represented.

The S3! leadership team introduced themselves and let attendees know that posters about our work were on display for their viewing and that the team would be on hand to answer questions. The circle then dispersed for food and fellowship and transitioned into an open-house atmosphere as people came and went throughout the evening.

The next day began at 9:00 a.m. in the same community center space where we had hosted the previous evening's gathering. Elayne Dorsey, the Kellogg Foundation fellow who had served as a research consultant on the project, agreed to come down to facilitate the one-day workshop. The girls were charged with devising an after-school project that they wanted to work on throughout the year. The morning was filled with interactive exercises that helped our group understand the meanings of community leadership and the importance of community power in social justice change. The afternoon shifted to identifying a topic for our yearlong project.

One topic that emerged among many was the dumpster issue. According to the girls, College Town, along with the town's Department of Housing, had decided to remove two dumpsters from the neighborhood to centralize garbage pickup. This caused hardship for some of the residents because it forced them to walk about the length of a city block up a steep hill to take out the household garbage.

Some residents launched a silent revolt by placing garbage in the empty space where the dumpsters had once stood. Other residents decided to speak up. The girls told me that in both cases, some of the residents, including their parents, had been threatened with eviction notices if they continued their protests. There were stories of housing officials going through the trash to identify residents who were waging the protests.

All the adult allies in the collective from "outside" the community immediately saw the dumpster issue as an important way to mobilize community-based power. This was an opportunity to work against the "capillary" forces of state power, as Foucault (1977) says, that reach into citizens' lives in public housing neighborhoods through the actions of "street-level bureaucrats" (Lipsky, 1980) who run housing departments and are free to retract resources and threaten residents' livelihoods. Often such actions are tied to neoliberal discourses of social responsibility anchored by legitimizing beliefs about who is or is not deserving of resources. Ultimately, these discourses render large numbers of people "arrestable, incarcerable, disposable, displaceable, and deportable" (Lipsitz, 2012, p. 1806).[8]

However, while the girls saw the dumpster issue as important—after all, they had witnessed their parents' humiliation and intimidation at the hands of the housing department—they were reluctant to take on this issue. They didn't verbalize their refusal (or perhaps the allies from outside the community didn't hear it), but it was there, hidden in plain sight, as the girls got behind the idea of having some sort of neighborhood party or perhaps starting a business, including such playful ideas as puppy washing. In the end, after much deliberation, and through a process made urgent by a paid consultant provided through a university grant, the collective decided to take on the Dumpster Project.

.   .   .   .   .

After the August 2007 retreat, there was a bustle of activity over the next two months as the girls organized into teams to "take on town hall" with regard to the dumpster issue. The group had shifted to seven regulars (Vanessa, Jade, Chantel, D'Misha, Yvonne, Tracey, and Taliah), paired with adult allies (myself; my student, Jenn Mease; and Stacey Craig, the young activist running the after-school programs at the Family Resource Center). There were three youth-adult teams assigned to lead three areas of action: (a) interviewing town officials to document the history of the decision, (b) interviewing residents to document waste disposal problems, and (c) organizing the community for action through popular education training. The teams met on their own to do their projects, and the whole group came together at the center once a week at dinnertime to provide updates and plan next steps. The caterer from the community gathering on the first night of the retreat had agreed to prepare a one-dish hot meal and bring it to our meetings each week.

Some of the girls stopped showing up for their team project meetings but almost always came to the weekly meetings. This fact was not lost on some of the adults and a couple of the girls, who all tied that attendance pattern to the weekly meals we enjoyed. My queries to the girls during our dinnertime team meetings, including a group exercise about accountability (we pledged to each be responsible to the success of the team), didn't change that pattern of attendance. I wondered whether and how this was related to the girls' path to agency.

Vanessa, who had quickly emerged as a leader among the girls, was on my team and led a phone interview with one of the town officials, an engineer at the Department of Public Works. She was brilliant! Later, when it was time to do the follow-up with the director of engineering, she refused to go. "Dr. Parker," she said, "I don't want to talk to a bunch of White people who won't change anything anyway." I went alone because I didn't want to cancel the meeting. I was equipped with the concerns that residents had shared with the S3! teams.

Vanessa's refusal in that moment and the other girls' reluctance to attend their project team meetings were clues from the girls—clues that were beginning to sink in. These refusals gestured at the hidden transcripts of their lives that were necessary for survival under the tight surveillance of housing policies, heavy policing, and seemingly constant scrutiny. For example, in the neighborhood context, direct confrontation with those in the White power structure seldom led to anything besides more trouble.

By about mid-October, most of the girls had lost interest in the project, and some of the residents started to question me about whether the housing department knew that it was in fact my students and I who were leading this project, rather than adults in the neighborhood.

That November 2007, we shifted our focus to planning a year-end celebration. Ms. Vergie had the idea of giving certificates to each of the girls and also certain parents, such as the dad who was vigilant about waiting with his child and other kids at the bus stop. The celebration took place in December at Stacey's house. It was a kind of open house that was filled with joy as all the girls, Ms. Delores, Ms. Vergie, and a few of the parents joined in for food, fun, and fellowship. Ms. Delores mentioned the Dumpster Project and the fact that one of the town officials had said rather emphatically at a recent meeting she had attended that the issue of "the dumpsters at Regal Gardens and University Heights is closed!" I chimed in that that was a sign of progress: when people start making those kinds of declarations from positions of power, it's a sign that they feel their power being threatened. In the back of my mind, though, I knew that the youth and their parents felt the matter was closed as well. What was supposed to be our (at least) yearlong project, from September 2007 through May of 2008, ended with our holiday party that December.

A PRIMER ON RADICAL LISTENING
TO CREATE "FREE SPACES"

After the Dumpster Project, it was clear that our community-based collective was not the *community-driven* partnership for social justice that we had envisioned from the start. Although it was the girls in the S3! leadership group who had identified the dumpster issue as an urgent community need, it was really those of us from outside the community who had the most energy and excitement about "taking on city hall" to confront the problem. To *us*, it seemed that challenging the decision to remove the dumpsters from Regal Gardens was an issue that would reveal the political control (town ordinances and housing department mandates) that nullified community voices. We thought it could also serve as a way to unify the neighbors in University Heights and Regal Gardens into a political coalition to build community power.

But we, the outside allies, missed how the "common sense" of survival in the community was influencing the girls, their families, and their neighbors. We missed the urgency of context in the route to social justice activism. A question guiding this chapter's analysis is pertinent here: *What motivates individual routes to social justice leadership given the conditions of extreme capitalism?* Ella Baker's praxis points to two radical listening practices that are lessons learned from the Dumpster Project about motivations to participate in social justice leadership. First, we needed to listen for context. Our collective's relational and knowledge-producing processes needed to consider the structural conditions that differently positioned community members and the allies from outside the community. Second, we needed to develop the capacity to listen from all those angles, given how that context enabled or constrained capacities for individualized routes to collective consciousness for social justice action.

The spaces in which the girls at University Heights and Regal Gardens spent their days were complex and plural. More than physical locations, the spaces the girls navigated were neighborhood zones, school zones, and elsewhere zones—in poet Claudia Rankine's words, "zoned for an encounter" (2014, p. 140). These spaces were informed by the daily interplay between raced, gendered, and classed urban life and the complex dynamics of im/migration, employment, housing, and the criminal justice system. Black girls and their mothers, grandmothers, aunts, and other women in segregated, urban, low-income communities often live with the constant threat of surveillance and control; they are often overpoliced and underprotected (Crenshaw, 2013).

Thinking in terms of this local context, the Dumpster Project had begun to expose some of the surveillance and control mechanisms at work at University Heights and Regal Gardens. And it also made the girls themselves visible. It made them dubious—based on their grounded and situated knowledge of how things work—that "taking on" the bureaucracy or even "speaking out" against it and "confronting" it would accomplish much good or any transformation. The idea that these tactics would succeed came from a position of privilege. Public housing for decades has been a site for African American women's struggle against inequality. It is a place that has lured academics, social workers, civil rights workers, antipoverty organizers, and Black power activists, all seeking to engage residents in the fight for social justice (Williams, 2004). Sometimes missing from analyses of African American women and girls, especially those living in poverty, is their struggle for citizenship: to be respected as girls and women in their own right. There is a disciplining narrative at work, what Crenshaw calls "the structural and discursive abandonment of women of color" (2013, p. 35). In popular culture, there are certain legitimizing beliefs pertaining to the "presumed dysfunction of women in need of discipline . . . [and] the normalization of their socioeconomic marginality alongside the renewed fantasies of gender normativity." These are "key elements sustaining the beliefs that 'people with problems are problems'" (Crenshaw, 2013, p. 35).

In telling this story of context, some parts of the story come from my witnessing fragments of the girls' lives and some come from the girls during our workshops and in focus-group interviews. I weave in these two angles of vision to simulate the process by which the girls' sense of agency came into view for me, if sometimes only momentarily. Baker's philosophy of meeting people where they are gestures toward that kind of ephemerality. Sometimes the hidden transcripts of subalternity are intended to be accessed, other times not.

The main challenge for our collective (although I don't think I realized it was a challenge in the beginning) was holding in view the adverse, immediate material conditions vulnerable youth face—the structural context of poverty, racism, and sexism—and at the same time *actually* being guided by the commitments to principles in Baker's catalyzing leadership approach; in this instance, using tenaciously participative decision-making structures that tilt toward the least powerful in society. Listening to the silences means listening for those instances of uneasy relations.

In youth engagement work, a criticism is that nonprofits that inadvertently (or intentionally) advance the logics of neoliberalism ignore the context of youths' lives and focus instead on the "potential" of a happier future that volunteers believe is possible—if the youths just work hard enough (Eliasoph, 2013, p. 56). My formal role as a university researcher sometimes put me at odds with the organic process of grassroots, group-centered leadership. For example, with the Dumpster Project, I was placing a great deal of emphasis on an abstract conception of context ("race" and poverty cause inequality, and we have to fight it), while also emphasizing a kind of "professional collaboration" approach that did not really draw on participatory values. Our collective was not doing the kind of deep, radical listening that would allow us to hear the silences. We needed the collective capacity to hear a process that represented a legitimate way of knowing and doing social change—a process born out of a struggle and knowledge about how to survive the constant threat of structural violence.

During the workshops leading up to the Dumpster Project, the girls often shared with the group how important it was to have a space where they could speak their minds on important issues like the town's dumpster decision. Self-naming their group Striving Sisters Speak! (S3!) was a testament to that desire. At the same time, the Dumpster Project had shown all of us that context matters when it comes to speaking up. The girls' idea of "speaking up" wasn't synonymous with speaking up to "city hall." It mattered that Black teen girls in the United States are constantly grappling with their identities—as are teens everywhere—but in their case it is often under the tight surveillance of extreme capitalism and constant threats to basic security, such as safe and stable housing. Context complicates the idea that an organized structure is needed to productively mobilize local knowledge. What would an engagement approach look like that could retain the girls' original clarity about the project and provide resources that would further energize rather than stifle their motivation to move forward?

As we would later learn, these girls had situated knowledge that we ignored when we mapped on the formalities of the project. These girls knew how to get things done "under the radar" of state or school surveillance and the potential violence that comes with the kind of engagement or visibility we were envisioning. What role could we or I have played in supporting that capacity? How can that situated knowledge inform organizing for social justice leadership while also taking into account other angles of vision in the partnership?

The central idea of radical listening is to create "free spaces." Social justice collectives must recognize limitations and opportunities from *all* angles of vision—under or beyond "the heel" of a particular set of circumstances. Indeed, it was while we were doing the engagement work of organizing the Dumpster Project that we were learning what it means to "lead from under the heels of social injustice" and also how we as a collective were constituting meanings of oppression, inequality, and social justice leadership.

As mentioned in chapter 1, central to Ella Baker's philosophy of praxis is the idea of leadership as teaching. Within the context of organizational-community partnerships, catalyzing leadership reinterprets Baker's idea of "leadership as teaching and learning," to be inclusive of the complicated relationship between organizers and people in vulnerable communities. In Payne's (1989) interpretation (and perhaps Baker's), the focus was on creating free spaces for people in vulnerable communities learning about activism and then practicing it. It did not include ways to address the problem of hierarchy in the relationships between the outside organizers or researchers and people in vulnerable communities. The Dumpster Project revealed the need for "building a readiness to learn" in the whole collective (Kellogg Foundation, 2007).

In retrospect, this issue was evident during the retreat to decide on the projects for that year, as well as while we were doing the projects. Each time an S3! member decided not to show up or speak up, and each time she did, was an opportunity for the entire collective to learn about leading from under the heels of social injustice. Each time one of the adult leaders became frustrated about a missed deadline or elated about a "success" that we would learn later was meaningless to the girls, was an opportunity for our collective to learn the limitations of an outsider's angle of vision and to listen to those silences, paradoxes, and frustrations as transcripts for collective action hidden in plain sight.

In the larger youth development literature, I think a predominant narrative about youth potential assumes what *should* be possible because, in the often-privileged position of "organizer" and "scholar-activist," we can easily imagine what *could* be possible. What became evident through the Dumpster Project is that the knowledge of what *is* possible from the grassroots is found in the silences, paradoxes, resistance to, and decisions in favor of action that emerge from the perspectives of those with their necks under the heels of power and injustice. Ella Baker said, "Strong people don't need strong leaders" (Cantarow, 1980, p. 53). Girls living under the heels of oppression need the space to see how their situated knowledge informs their capacity to lead. Adult allies need to trust the collective process that allows that to happen. This kind of trust among people at the grassroots and organizers-as-resources-and-allies is fundamental to the work of social justice leadership. It defines the space in which people step into their own sense of power. That attention to context happened through the CommUNITY Festival.

CREATING PARTICIPATIVE SPACES:
THE COMMUNITY FESTIVAL

We regrouped in January 2008. Elayne Dorsey, my contact from the Kellogg Foundation, had been in touch to see how we were doing, and I told her about the setback. She said that what had happened was not uncommon in youth-adult partnerships such as ours that are building readiness for social justice work. She invited a contingent from our collective to join the next national gathering of community organizations supporting youth activism at the Kellogg Leadership for Community Change (KLCC) initiative. The gathering was to be held in Boston in late March.

Using the last of my research funds, the Ella Baker Women's Center group traveled to Boston: two S3! leaders, Taliah and Vanessa (who had never been on a plane); two students, Joaquín (who was now back in New York at the New School, finishing out his senior year) and Alyssa (a service-learning student); and two adult allies, Ms. Vergie and I. This would be the first of several networking trips to see how other youth of color were doing social justice leadership in their communities.

In Boston, we were among seventy-five people representing five groups from across the country. Most of the attendees were executive directors and staff—including youth leaders—at nonprofit organizations such as the Boys and Girls Clubs of Benton Harbor, Michigan.

The networking trip to Boston was especially transformative for our group. During our breakout sessions, Vanessa and Taliah shared their experience attempting to do the Dumpster Project and learned how other multigenerational groups were operating in their communities, including youth and adults at Roca (the Rock), a community center in the Chelsea area of greater Boston that was serving Latinx and recent immigrant families. The girls attended a workshop and learned a new communication tool for discovering community needs for further action: the "fishbone" process. This is a tool in the Six Sigma quality improvement business model, intended to reduce the number of defects in manufacturing systems. KLCC had marshaled it to support communities that wanted to identify root causes of community problems.

.   .   .   .   .

When Vanessa and Taliah returned to College Town, inspired by what they had learned, they wanted to do a workshop using the fishbone tool. There was positive buzz in the neighborhood about the girls traveling to Boston, so we decided to capitalize on that energy to plan the workshop right away. The workshop was held on a cool April evening at the Family Resource Center in the heart of Regal Gardens. All eight girls from the summer workshop were in attendance, as well as Stacey, Alyssa, and I. In addition, several of the mothers were in attendance: Ms. Dorita, Ms. Lynetta, and Ms. Naomi. These women were already becoming highly engaged allies and part of the center collective.

Emerging from the workshop led by Taliah and Vanessa was the idea for an event to be called the CommUNITY Festival. The festival was to focus attention on the real concerns in the community: overpolicing and the need to build unity among residents so that they don't rely on the police to resolve disputes.

Of course this is precisely what the girls had suggested as a project focus in the August 2007 workshops. They had wanted to have some sort of community party instead of doing the Dumpster Project. But the "organizers" hadn't been listening.

Deciding to organize and hold the festival was a major assertion of community power, and the girls were the reason it was happening. Once the momentum gathered, members from both the University Heights and Regal Gardens neighborhoods grew energized about making the festival happen. In June 2008, Vanessa and Taliah helped to co-organize the S3! leadership workshops, working alongside Stacey, me, Jenn, and Alyssa, now a MURAP research intern, as Joaquín and Elisa had been the previous summer. Two of the original eight S3! girls had moved away, but two more joined as core members (Taylor and Tania), keeping our core S3! team at eight.

Initially we met at the space at EmPOWERment and maintained our structural focus on personal, organizational, and community leadership. Vanessa, Taliah, Taylor, Tania, and Yvonne were the most active members and rotated leading the critical arts activities in the curriculum. Jenn and Stacey also hosted birthday celebrations and other fun gatherings for the girls at their respective apartments to support the bonding that was beginning to take shape among them. This bonding seems to be the crucial prerequisite to caring in any kind of voluntary activity. Without either the requirement to participate or the joy of participating, the voluntary, optional activities are the first to go. By mid-July the primary focus was on organizing the festival.

We shifted our meetings to the center in the community and maintained a flexible meeting structure to accommodate the growing collective. We helped the S3! girls organize five teams that would follow our youth-adult partnership structure. Jenn Mease was especially influential in this phase, coaching the girls to share their ideas as they settled on the five areas of festival planning: fundraising, games, food, program, and logistics. There would be a talent show, a spoken-word group from the university, and representatives from the town council. Everyone agreed that the main activities for the festival (food, bounce house, and main stage) should be staged "up top," as the residents referred to the University Heights neighborhood. With this location, the street that separated University Heights and Regal Gardens would have to be closed. This would not only create more safety but also be a major symbol of unity between the two neighborhoods. According to Ms. Lynetta, a longtime resident of Regal Gardens, the relations between the two communities had been more distant in recent years, likely because of the regular police presence in Regal Gardens. It would also create the capacity for people to walk freely between Regal Gardens and University Heights to create a festival atmosphere. We established October 21 as the date for what we decided would be the first annual CommUNITY Festival.

In late August, as College Town officials heard about the festival, I found myself being called in by officials who wanted to make sure that I was aware of what was going on "down there." "Does housing know about this?" the director of transportation asked me when I called on behalf of residents to request some large orange construction barrels to shut down the street that divided the two neighborhoods. Somehow the police chief got wind of the festival planning and emailed to alert me to the danger that I probably was not aware of awaiting me in the neighborhood. He asked if I was aware of the constant feuding between residents in University Heights and Regal Gardens. He wondered if there were plans in place for police security. The town officials were revealing to me the disciplining narratives that fueled all the feelings of vulnerability to state power among residents.

I did not respond to the chief's message. Instead, I printed the message and shared it with Vanessa and her mother, Ms. Dorita, whose whole family, including Vanessa's stepdad Darnell and little brothers Sammy and Michael, were all now involved with the planning. Vanessa said she would include the chief's message on that week's festival planning meeting agenda.

At the festival planning meeting the following week, there was a hushed silence as Vanessa read aloud the police chief's email. Moments earlier, the room had been bustling with talk of games that would be best suited for different age ranges, a talent show to showcase neighborhood talent, and, of course, food. The room was filled to capacity with an intergenerational group of community members: younger kids who were on task teams to organize the games, several of the girls' mothers, and Darnell. All were from Regal Gardens and University Heights, the two communities that the chief was warning me about in his email.

After Vanessa had finished reading the chief's email, she spoke up first. "Who is he talking about?" she asked. Then her mother spoke: *"Certainly not anyone in this room!"* Then came a deluge of voices, indignant that someone from the outside could talk about the community in that way. I wondered aloud if the chief had ever been to the neighborhood. "No," someone said. The *police* had been to the neighborhood, perhaps a hundred times, but never the police chief and never by the community's invitation. Everyone agreed that the chief should come see for himself what people in the community were planning. I responded to the chief's email the next day with an invitation to meet with the planning team.

The chief arrived in the neighborhood on a sunny September afternoon (after he had first dispatched an unmarked patrol car to drive through the neighborhood). It was just after the kids got home from school. The community was filled with laughter as kids played in the street that meandered through the 1970s-style brick apartments. The community organizing collective, which had grown to include more community members and girls, was gathered around the table in the center. At the table were Ms. Naomi (Jade's and Chantel's aunt), Ms. Lynetta (Tania's mom), Moni (Naomi's seven-year-old daughter), Natalie (age sixteen, who was just joining the group), Jade (age seventeen), myself, Stacey, and Joaquín, who was now back at the university as a first-year graduate student and continuing as an Ella Baker Women's Center volunteer.

The chief came in, and after everyone had introduced themselves, Ms. Naomi began to tell him about our plans for the festival. As the chief stood before us, his gun protruded from his holster. Seven-year-old Moni, who was standing beside him, suddenly looked up at him and asked, "Why do you have a gun?"

I think he said something about it being part of his uniform or something like that. But it was a statement that did some work in the moment. My sense was that the gun was out of place. This was a neighborhood, a community, a place different from what the police chief had probably imagined. After that, the police chief walked the neighborhood with the group, with Moni leading the way up the hill to the place where we would stage the festival. At that point, the chief had become part of the planning. He suggested ways to set up the various sites for the games and understood, finally, that this was something the community wanted. To be sure, this was a momentary victory—the police chief was part of the process and participating in the creation of a different narrative about the community—but that is not what this story is primarily about. This story is about a route for communities to see their own power—even if it is momentary—and about building community muscle memory.

The festival was to happen on the day of a big game between the university and the University of Georgia, a chief opponent in the athletic conference. Yet because of the ground that had been tilled by the girls' interactions with town officials during the Dumpster Project, and now having secured the chief of police as an advocate, Ms. Naomi and I managed to lobby to get the town to close down the street that separated the two neighborhoods so that community members could walk freely between the two spaces. This was accomplished without the "permission" of the town's housing department. In fact, the whole festival happened without any engagement with the housing department. The local housing department's assumed authority to give "permission" to the residents to have a street festival was countered when the CommUNITY Festival was planned outside of that presumed authority. This was a moment when the girls "knew better" and had more common *and* good sense about which power structures to avoid entirely based on past experience. It was our first glimpse of the Bakerian principle, "strong people don't need strong leaders," enacted in our work, illustrating how strong communities can devise their own solutions. The girls knew that staying under the radar of bureaucratic surveillance and administrative regimes—going around, not through—would work, and once everyone heeded that knowledge, the event was all set.

Figure 3. Chanelle and Kiesha at the first annual CommUNITY Festival at Regal Gardens and University Heights. Photo by author.

On the day of the festival, the whole neighborhood was bustling with energy. Arthur Romano, a local peace activist who had formerly lived near University Heights and Regal Gardens, brought a large white wooden board and paints for residents and other attendees to create a community mural (see figure 3). Arthur would later join the collective as a key co-organizer and ally. Ms. Dorita had hired a man with a barbecue pit, which he pulled behind a big gas-guzzling car from the 1970s, in some ways symbolizing the community's nostalgic hope to reclaim all that is productive from the past, while facing the hard work of excavating the complicated legacies from that past to accomplish a more socially just present and future. The man set up the barbecue pit at the top of the parking lot, away from the inflatable gym but not far from the place where the talent show would be staged.

S3! leaders had created bright green flyers that read, "This is OUR Community!" One side was filled with the agenda for the day, including Vanessa and Antonio (Naomi's son) serving as MCs, a spoken-word group from the university, a College Town council member, food, and games. The other side had affirmations about liberation, including the quote from Ella Baker, "Strong people don't need strong leaders," declaring the CommUNITY Festival to be a demonstration of community power.

Neighbors mingled, laughed, and played. One can imagine Ella Baker, as a teen at Shaw University, or later as an activist in the 1960s, coming to College Town and being welcomed into this vibrant neighborhood space.

.   .   .   .   .

After the CommUNITY Festival, our collective had a celebration and reflection gathering to evaluate our latest project and think about where we would go next. The girls were excited about the prospect of having more events in the community, and someone mentioned planning an election night party, given then candidate Barack Obama's historic candidacy. This generated a great deal of excitement, and we intended to plan it. In the meantime, the girls had two opportunities to speak at university-sponsored events at the invitation of sociologist Judith Blau. The first was at her social movements class, where Taliah, Jade, and Vanessa gave a talk about youth-led organizing, based on their experience leading the CommUNITY Festival. The second was at a Human Rights Week event at a local community center, at which several S3! girls, along with Moni, gave a presentation on Ella Baker's legacy of community organizing. Naomi also attended the event, along with Joaquín and me. Two other S3! leaders had begun working with me on a university research grant project (see chapter 4). Through these activities, there was a sense that our collective was strengthening our bonds and building our capacity to act.

On the night of the election, the Family Resource Center was bustling with activity. Stacey, the public allies fellow who was running the after-school program for middle schoolers, had created a US map so that the younger kids could draw in "red" and "blue" states as the results came in. Earlier in the week she had given a brief teach-in on the election process. The older youth had helped plan the snacks, drinks, and music, as it was decided that the night would have a party atmosphere, and people could drop in and out. The feelings of expectancy and hope at the center were palpable. The whole room erupted into cheers as the election was called and Barack Obama was announced as the forty-fourth president of the United States—the first African American US president.

More incredible news followed election night. The press release announcing the news that S3! would be heading to Washington, DC for President Obama's inauguration captured the excitement of the time:

UNC professor, youth leaders to celebrate Obama inauguration in Washington, DC

CHAPEL HILL—The e-mail professor Patricia Parker received shortly after New Year's Day seemed like a dream. She and members of the Chapel Hill-based youth action group that she founded were invited to join in festivities at the JW Marriott hotel in Washington, DC, to help celebrate the presidential inauguration on Jan. 20—for free.

Parker, a communication studies professor at the University of North Carolina at Chapel Hill, is the founder of the Ella Baker Women's Center for Leadership and Community Activism. The flagship project of Parker's non-profit is Striving Sisters Speak!!! (S^3), a group of young women of color in low-income neighborhoods who are working to create coalitions of social justice in their communities.

Five high school women and several volunteers and chaperones with the group will attend a celebration to commemorate the Inauguration thanks to The Stafford Foundation's People's Inauguration Project and other UNC donors. They will attend a prayer breakfast, a luncheon at which Martin Luther King III will speak, and an inaugural ball, among other festivities.

—UNC–Chapel Hill news release (January 2009)

Ms. Dorita was the first person I called with the news that January morning. "This is huge!!!" I said. She agreed. We all gathered at her house to plan the trip. One important aspect was prepping the girls for the media spotlight they were about to enter. We discussed the potential for exploitation and the need to control when and where we would give interviews. It was agreed that I would be the point person with the media, then consult with Ms. Dorita, Ms. Naomi, and Ms. Lynetta before arranging any media junkets. We also agreed to practice the interviews beforehand and, when possible, to follow a script, of which those being interviewed would have final approval. I became their agent and media handler. The girls were excited, if a bit nervous, but they left the meeting knowing that they were under no obligation to submit to any interviews. The evidence of that right to refusal appeared when they chose not to do an interview when they first arrived in Washington, DC (tired and hungry), to the chagrin of one of the local news anchors.

After receiving the inauguration invitation, the girls enthusiastically chose to accept the opportunity to open College Town's council meeting on January 12, 2009. When I told them about the opportunity, I emphasized that this was their chance to speak and declare themselves as representatives of College Town at the inauguration of the first Black president of the United States. I had the sense that the girls understood the importance of speaking into a politicized space, a White space usually zoned for their absence. They seemed to grasp the power of entering that space at this moment in history and on their own terms. They insisted on writing their own introduction speeches, which I didn't hear until the night of the presentation. They spoke with power and grace. Kennedy, whose family had recently moved to the neighborhood, was among the first girls to speak: "My name is Kennedy Stokely. I started working with S3! in August, after my family moved to Regal Gardens, and I have enjoyed every part of it. I'm very excited about going to President-elect Barack Obama's inauguration. I'm proud to be a community organizer just like him." Kennedy's reference to the fact that both she and President Obama were community organizers is one she would later repeat in press interviews and in conversations I overheard. As each girl spoke in turn, the positive energy in the room was palpable. We all beamed with that energy as we posed for pictures in front of the rows of photographs of former council members (all White men) (see figure 4).

One important aspect of the trip to Washington, DC that reinforced our developing model was the opportunity for the young women of S3! to network with members of the four other youth groups that had been invited by the Stafford Foundation. Stacey and Alyssa, who made the trip to Washington as volunteers and chaperones, would accompany the girls to the youth social justice networking night during the "People's Inauguration," where they first learned about the juvenile justice efforts in New York to change laws about locking up sixteen- and seventeen-year-old children in adult detention centers and prisons. This terrible injustice had been halted in all but two states: New York and North Carolina. The trip to President Obama's first inauguration turned out to

Figure 4. S3! speaks before the College Town Council, January 2009. Photo by Stacey Craig.

be a spark that would help ignite one of S3!'s future campaigns, discussed in chapter 4.

PRIMER ON CRITICAL DIALOGIC GROUP PROCESS: TILTING TOWARD THE LEAST POWERFUL

The lessons learned from the Dumpster Project about listening to context and silence and from all angles catalyzed our collective to plan the community-driven CommUNITY Festival project and resulted in the subsequent strengthening of our collective. In learning that the girls had no interest in the Dumpster Project per se, but that they were indeed energized at the prospect of unifying the community as a prerequisite to community power, we had tended to one of the central questions in community-based organizing: What motivates individual routes to social justice leadership given the conditions of extreme capitalism? We learned to meet girls on their terms, creating the space for *their* motivations to drive the CommUNITY Festival project. However, we still needed to determine how to accomplish a high level of participation, in which everyone is taking part and accountable to the collective success. That challenge was at the heart of the second central question guiding this chapter: What would truly participative spaces look like, in which productive knowledge could emerge from all angles of vision and from people at various stages of becoming socially conscious?

In organizational leadership theory, participative decision-making has been defined traditionally in terms of management "allowing" workers to have a say in decisions, often without a deep questioning of managerial control (Deetz, 1992). Alternatively, in organization-community partnerships, as informed by Ella Baker's philosophy of praxis, participative decision-making must begin with a deep and radical (status quo questioning) analysis of how structural power is circulating through us and the community. In her view, participatory structures were necessary for fighting interpersonal, systemic, and other forms of structural violence (James, 1994; Ransby, 2003). To that end, the members of our collective were intentional about creating a critical dialogic process and also using tenaciously participative decision-making that tilts toward community expertise, since it was their lives at stake.

In the planning of the CommUNITY Festival, we used the same structure that we had for the Dumpster Project (three S3! leaders partnered with one adult; we held weekly meetings at which teams shared updates). However, we added to that commitment an intentional focus on decentering the power of the adult allies. As a mentor of young activists leading 1960s social justice movements, Ella Baker had the capacity to hold a space wherein youth activists' voices were centered, as many of the more well-known anecdotes about her reveal. There is an oft-cited anecdote about Baker sitting for hours listening to SNCC activists debate a particular tactic, only at critical points joining the conversation to ask a question that transformed the conversation in a productive way. Baker provided this context for the anecdote: "Most of the youngsters had been trained to believe in or to follow adults. . . . I felt they ought to have a chance to learn to think things through and to make the decisions" (Cantarow, 1980, p. 87). In that spirit, we used a critical dialogic process that involved teaching and supporting group facilitation capacities in our now-expanding collective, supporting a culture of trial and error with ideas and actions, incorporating circle processes that encouraged dialogue and sustained radical listening, and rotating leadership roles to decenter individual power. We also held formal and informal discussions about different kinds of expertise that informed our collective's work.

As a central part of our process, we had an S3! leader codevelop meeting agendas and rotated roles for each meeting (facilitator, notetaker, and timekeeper). Vanessa, Jenn, and Joaquín developed a standard agenda that could be tweaked depending on the emergent topic that week. Our collective had to grow in our commitment to using these communicative processes and making them work for us. People within the community would call out others for not adhering to the process—an important sign that the process was working. We carried this critical dialogic process forward into the next phase of our work, and it helped us constitute participative spaces for our growing collective.

As Baker's philosophy of praxis teaches, adult allies in the group could not "check ourselves" unless we were willing to think critically about how power was enabling or constraining participation. To that end, and especially after the lessons of the Dumpster Project, we knew our collective's social justice work needed to develop the capacity for sustained radical listening. More specifically, we needed to develop together a group structure that enabled the capacity to listen closely to how the girls interpreted and countered the narratives circulating within and around them and how these narratives informed their choices about activism, then tilt the decision-making power toward them. After all, their lives were the ones that could be threatened or changed, as demonstrated in some of the residents' earlier attempts to protest the dumpster issue. The girls and their community-based allies did not make *all* the decisions about the CommUNITY Festival. However, the ones they did make—about the visit from the police chief and the decision to hold the festival in the first place—were a critical assertion of community power that had not been seen in a long time. They were decisions made on their own terms and in their own time.

.   .   .   .   .

The participatory process calls attention to the immediacy of place: What do we want to create together? Why? Why now? It also challenges all participants to consider how each of us is complicit in reinforcing the very structures that might hinder our work. Ella Baker's catalyzing leadership approach calls on us to develop the collective capacity not only to remove the obstacles to community voice in organizational-community partnerships but also to cocreate participatory spaces. These spaces can attend to productive knowledge and expertise that come from all angles and point us along the route to collective consciousness and activism. The next chapter builds on that foundation to explore how catalyzing leadership can scale up to broaden its impact.

4 "Strong People Don't Need Strong Leaders"

ENGAGING SOCIAL JUSTICE STORYTELLING
FOR CATALYTIC LEADERSHIP

So far this case study has analyzed two commitments that flow from Ella Baker's catalytic leadership approach: to community power and to group-centered leadership. Those commitments are fulfilled through communication capacities that build organizational-community partnerships and through the creation of participative spaces that catalyze individual routes to collective consciousness and social justice activism. This chapter presents the third and final commitment, exposing the workings of structural power through the strategic actions of counter-storytelling communities (Bell et al., 2008). Baker's often-quoted mantra that "strong people don't need strong leaders" suggests that communities can not only see their power but also deploy it for higher social justice aims that disrupt the status quo. This chapter is about how that power is deployed through storytelling, critical arts, and performance pedagogies and by keeping an eye on coactive spaces in which social justice storytelling can do the most transformative work (see table 4).

Coactive spaces (see chapter 2), as Follett described them, are created through interactive processes and methods "by which desires may interweave" to yield something new from old, seemingly intractable conflicts (1924, p. xiv). Critical pedagogies that use poetry, visual art, and perfor-

Table 4 Engaging Social Justice Storytelling for Catalytic Leadership
Commitment, Problem, and Communication Practices

Commitment	Problem	Communication Practices
Expose the workings of structural power: "Strong people don't need strong leaders." (Baker 1980)	**Broadening social impact:** problems of coalition building to realize political and economic impact	• Critical pedagogies for creating counter-storytelling communities: 　○ Storytelling for social justice framework 　○ Coactive service-learning classrooms 　○ Popular education/performance • Joining or creating coactive spaces for social justice storytelling: 　○ Convening conferences 　○ Hosting forums 　○ Creating counter-storytelling art

mance are essential for creating coactive spaces. However, whether and how counter-storytelling communities develop is a highly contingent and multilayered process.

As you read through this chapter, consider how you might address the following questions in your work: How do communities develop into "storytelling" communities of resistance to create counternarratives to those that circulate in and around them? Where are the places for people living under the heel of injustice to narrate their lives as a way of disrupting and transforming state–corporate power?

These questions became compelling ones for the Ella Baker Women's Center after our collective's success with the CommUNITY Festival in October 2008. The girls of S3! were now firmly established as the flagship youth leadership program at the center. They seemed ready to build on the momentum of their success. Some productive tensions remained around the girls' desire to participate on their own terms. Our collective of youth and adult allies in the neighborhood, the university, and the surrounding community had slowed our pace so as to engage with those tensions as we moved forward.

Thinking about where and how S3! would focus their organizing efforts next allowed our collective to engage more directly with the range of critical pedagogies underlying our social justice curriculum. It also reoriented and broadened our work within the Regal Gardens and University Heights neighborhoods and led us to find other coactive spaces, such as the CommUNITY Festival, in which the girls could advance social justice leadership.

.   .   .   .   .

Three critical pedagogical frameworks were helpful in deepening and broadening the impact of the center's work with the girls and their allies: the storytelling for social justice framework, community-engaged service-learning classrooms, and the Theatre of the Oppressed.

The storytelling for social justice framework (Bell, 2010; Bell et al., 2008) emphasizes the use of poetry, visual arts, media, performance, and other critical pedagogies for creating and sharing stories. The framework utilizes storytelling at the personal, group, community, and national levels to expose structural power and catalyze broader political action.

Through the application of critical arts pedagogies and critical race curricula, groups can excavate four intricately related story types (stock stories, concealed stories, resistance stories, and emerging/transforming stories) to cocreate counter-storytelling communities in which stories about power— including race, racism, and antiracism—can be "openly shared, respectfully heard, and critically discussed/analyzed" (Bell, 2010, p. 20).

Briefly, *stock stories* are the public and ubiquitous stories in dominant mainstream institutions, such as schools, government, workplaces, and the media.[1] These are stories told by the dominant group, as constructed, for example, through race, gender, sexuality, and ability. The dominant stories are passed on through historical and literary documents and celebrated through public rituals, monuments, and media representations. *Concealed stories* coexist alongside stock stories and often provide a very different perspective. Concealed stories are those of subalternity and often remain in the shadows, hidden from public view. For example, acts of police harassment and intimidation in communities of color stand in stark contrast to some police departments' motto to promise to "protect and serve" communities. Concealed stories may be told and retold by people on the margins or may remain hidden. Their work continues either way; they productively challenge and deconstruct stock stories for social justice aims that are passed on from generation to generation.[2] But untold concealed stories may also work to sustain intergenerational trauma, if they are never tended to, or they may work to stigmatize people who are marginalized, if they are deployed to achieve oppressive political aims. For example, amid the ruins of poverty that extreme capitalism often leaves in its wake are people suffering from drug addiction or living with domestic violence. The root causes of these conditions are often concealed, while victim-blaming stories about them are deployed to feed neoconservative political strategies.

The third story type is *resistance stories*. Ella Baker's bridge leadership, described in chapter 1, is a good example of how concealed stories become resistance stories. It epitomizes how people have resisted racism, challenged the stock stories that support it, and fought for more equal and inclusive social arrangements. Resistance stories often catalyze new, perhaps germinal stories, but gesturing toward community power. The fourth and final type, *emerging/transforming stories*, takes shape as communities build on those histories of resistance. Emerging stories are catalyzing when they fuel counter-storytelling communities that "challenge the stock stories, build on and amplify concealed and resistance stories, and create new stories to interrupt the status quo and energize change" (Bell, 2010, p. 25). They are new stories that are deliberately constructed in a particular moment (see chapter 1). These stories reflect a collective's capacity to see its power and enable new possibilities for social justice action, as happened for S3! and their adult allies after the first annual CommUNITY Festival in 2008.

From the beginning, the work of our burgeoning collective was about creating counternarratives. In an inversion of the storytelling for social justice model, we began with an orientation to stories that would directly contradict the status quo, norming stories about crime, lack of individual accountability, and the need to discipline women of color that circulated in College Town and were reinforced in popular culture narratives about predominantly Black neighborhoods. As outsiders to the community, my students and I were continually orienting our work to listen for concealed stories told by the girls, other community members, student-service learners, and staff at the center. Through our workshops, in small groups, and sitting on the stoop in the neighborhood, our collective was developing the capacity to listen to silences and to adapt our organization based on what we heard. These were truths spoken among ourselves to challenge (national and personally held) beliefs about public housing that politicized and racialized the neighborhood and produced negative labels that stuck to people's identities at school, work, and play (Block, 2008).

For example, one crisp fall afternoon in October 2008, I sat outside talking with Ms. Eliza, an octogenarian who lived in Regal Gardens. She shared an encounter she had had on a local bus with a fellow rider: "It was a friendly conversation. She was a nice lady and we were just talking, you know, about the weather and other pleasantries. At one point I mentioned that I lived in Regal Gardens. Then she said, 'Oh! You live down there?' I said, 'Yes I do! And I love it!' Seeing the look on her face was what was so disturbing—as if Regal Gardens was just the worst place. We didn't talk anymore after that."

Ms. Eliza's story reveals meanings and labels that were always there— sometimes concealed or held at bay, but present nonetheless. I recall another conversation in Ms. Naomi's kitchen after S3! had met at her home for one of our CommUNITY Festival planning meetings. Naomi was an aunt to two S3! leaders, Jade and Chantel, and the mother of seven-year-old Moni, introduced in chapter 3. She was the girl who asked the provocative question of the town's police chief during a visit to the neighborhood. Naomi was also the mother of fifteen-year-old Antonio and thirteen-year-old Thomas. I was talking to Naomi and Antonio about the festival plans, and Antonio was full of ideas. Then the conversation turned to school. I asked how school was going for him. Antonio and his mother exchanged glances. There was so much that I saw in Antonio's sweet face that reminded me of my own teen-aged son's countenance—full of grace. But in that moment, I saw what seemed to be a tinge of shame as he recounted a story of being sent to in-school suspension (ISS) for talking in class when others were doing the same, but they were not singled out for ISS. This was one of the concealed stories: a young man is coming of age, feeling victimized at school, but perhaps feeling powerless even to understand that, let alone how to change it, and I'm standing there recognizing the pain and the wrongness, and it reinforces my commitment to work alongside people besieged by a capitalist-driven (the stock story), school-to-prison pipeline. Naomi saw it, too. In the years to come, I served as one of Naomi's confidants and allies as she documented and fought the targeting of her sons at their predominantly White high school. In that moment, the impulse to create a counter-story came from a deep certainty about the wrongness of the status quo.

The CommUNITY Festival (see chapter 3) was a resistance story, through which we began to develop counternarratives. It had emerged from community knowledge and sparked momentum for counternarratives to reveal what could become a reality for the community. The girls of S3! identified what they saw as a community need: to rebuild relationships in the neighborhood as a way of supporting activities for older youth in the community. The festival also helped fuel a growing sense of collectivity in the community, a necessary precondition to collective action (Bhattacharyya, 2004). We were also strengthening the connections in the community-university partnership in ways that would broaden our impact on both sides of the hyphen.

. . . . .

In October 2008, as the center collective moved into the second year of its community-university partnership, we began to engage more directly with resources from the surrounding community and university. An important resource was Arthur Romano, the community-based peace activist who supplied the idea and materials for the community mural at the CommUNITY Festival. Arthur connected our group to local arts activists trained in popular education methodologies and critical arts activist pedagogies, including Romano's cotrainer, Cherine Badawi, based in Oakland, California, and a core team of local arts activists: Michael (Mikey) Irwin, an English teacher at Chapel Hill High School; Rachel Valentine, a community organizer and AmeriCorps fellow; and spoken-word artists, CJ Suitt and Kane Smego. Each of these allies helped the center collective incorporate critical arts pedagogies, such as poetry, drawing, and painting. Perhaps the most transforming critical arts practice we learned was the Theatre of the Oppressed, often referred to as "T.O." (Tee-Oh) by practitioners (Boal, 2005; Mandala Center for Change, n.d.; Santos, 2019).

T.O. is based on the ideas underlying the pedagogy of the oppressed, developed by Paulo Freire, the twentieth-century Brazilian educator and activist. Freire's (1970) pedagogy of the oppressed theorizes the productive use of *conscientizacao*, or consciousness-raising, for people living in and with oppressive histories. Similar to Ella Baker's philosophy and belief in the power of people in oppressed communities to lead social justice change, Freire argued for a process of *conscientizacao* and dialogue to build the capacity for people to "see" their oppression, "analyze" its root causes, and "act" to transform the social condition and end the oppression. Augusto Boal, influenced by Freire's work, incorporated theater and performance as a critical process to facilitate this triumvirate of seeing, acting, and analyzing. He theorized that theater and performance—not words or rote teaching— allow people to engage with trauma and the effects of oppression that linger in the body, often without the words to express their meanings. He drew many of his techniques from the work of Abdias do Nascimento, the Afro-Brazilian founder of Black Experimental Theatre. Boal's (2005) book, *Games for Actors and Non-Actors*, leads practitioners through movements, scenarios, games, and other activities that culminate in four theatrical systems for creating counter-storytelling communities: Image Theatre (using the body as "clay" to create images of experiences or desires for the future), Invisible Theatre (issue-oriented scenes to stimulate public dialogue), Forum Theatre (audience-driven problem-solving techniques for "rehearsal for the future"), and Legislative Theatre (Forum Theatre but with the purpose of proposing new laws to be passed).

T.O. is practiced around the world wherever collectives are challenging the status quo. Many of the practitioners (called "Jokers") are trained at the Center for Theatre of the Oppressed in Rio de Janeiro, Brazil, where some worked directly with Boal before his death in 2009. A typical T.O. workshop of ten to twenty people might begin with warm-up exercises in which participants begin to reflect on their embodied experiences with feelings of hope, despair, joy, or indifference. One exercise, called "filling a space," involves all participants walking through a bounded space (large room, outdoor garden, etc.) as the Joker shouts instructions on how to calibrate their pace. The instructions begin simply (e.g., "walk as if you're late for a meeting" or "imagine you're with a loved one on a stroll") and grow in complexity as the workshop develops ("secretly identify someone in the group and label them as your 'enemy' and another as your 'protector' and walk through the space to stay as far away from your enemy as possible, while staying as close to your protector as you can"). Participants are urged to reflect (during debrief periods or in their personal journals) about conflicting feelings that emerge (sometimes one's "enemy" is someone else's "protector"). These reflections become the foundation for scenes that are developed later and used in public forum theater performances at which audiences intervene to act out alternative endings for the scenes.

From 2009 through 2013, our collective actively incorporated T.O. systems and techniques, along with other critical arts pedagogies, to broaden our impact. However, in 2009 our group was immersed in T.O. training. In early January and later in April, we learned T.O. practices with Arthur, Michael, Rachel, and CJ. Those experiences came in conjunction with the service-learning course I created, which I discuss later. In the summer of 2009, two S3! leaders, Tawanna and Shana, who joined the group after the first CommUNITY Festival, also traveled with me to the historic Highlander Research and Education Center for their Seeds of Fire camp. The camp was grounded in T.O. praxis and turned out to be a transformative experience for all of us.

·   ·   ·   ·   ·

The Highlander Research and Education Center in New Market, Tennessee, has been a coactive space for social justice organizing since its inception in the 1930s and continues today as a vibrant center for catalyzing social justice leadership. Ella Baker participated in gatherings there, famously so in the 1960s, as the grassroots movements for nonviolent resistance to desegregation and voting rights campaigns were being organized, and she counseled the group to see that the two movements were not mutually exclusive.[3] The Seeds of Fire program at Highlander is a yearlong program that brings together southern and Appalachian youth-led and youth-centered groups and individuals organizing for social justice and change. At the time we attended, there were summer mini camps that focused on the importance of having youth cotrain and coeducate their communities and each other to catalyze systemic change back home and elsewhere. One of the most powerful experiences was a Forum Theatre performance that was adapted to provide youth with the tools to critically

Figure 5. Tawanna, third from left, participating in Forum Theatre at Seeds of Fire Camp. Photo by author.

examine economic inequality while making connections locally, region-ally, nationally, and transnationally.

The performance happened over the last two days of the seven-day camp. The fifty youth and adult participants were introduced to a timeline that corresponded to the root causes of global economic inequality that had developed over the past several hundred years, mapping shifts in the political economy that had resulted in forced migration, enslavement, and violence. The participants spent the first day learning about the cultures and histories of events on the timeline. The next day the participants formed small groups corresponding to particular time periods and used visual art, poetry, music, and dramatic performances to explore the root causes of problems in the context of the respective time periods. Tawanna (pictured in figure 5) was part of the group that powerfully demonstrated the statistics on shifts in income inequality in the United States during the mid- to late twentieth century and the widening gap between people located at the top and people increasingly impoverished or precariously close to poverty. According to the Economic Policy Institute, between 1979 and 2007, real income rose cumulatively by 240.5 percent among the top 1 percent of households in the United States, versus 71 percent for the 95th–99th income percentiles.[4] In Tawanna's group's simulation of concentration of wealth among the top 1 percent, a row of ten chairs was assembled to signify income wealth per household, with ten participants standing behind the chairs (as if income equality were represented by one chair per person). Then, as the dramatization began, one person representing the top 1 percent sprawled across nine of the chairs, while the remaining nine actors struggled to situate themselves on one chair, representing the remaining 99 percent of US households. During the discussion that followed, the youth and adult participants discussed how income inequality was evident in their communities and identified some of the root causes related to the disappearance of manufacturing jobs, lack of access to education and training, and immigration status.

.   .   .   .   .

In the fall of 2008, the university helped sustain the university-community partnership with a Robertson Grant award to support undergraduate research partnerships between UNC–Chapel Hill and Duke University. I cowrote the grant with Sherryl Broverman at the Global Health Institute at Duke, who was partnering with community leaders in Muhuru Bay, Kenya, to create a school for girls. One condition of the research grant was that students at our respective universities present their findings at a conference. Thus was born the idea for the Sharing the Mantle Conference for intergenerational leadership. It was shaped largely by S3!'s leadership of the CommUNITY Festival and the desire to share what we'd learned through that event with others. Writing the grant also inspired me to create a first-year seminar that would partner students in the seminar with S3! leaders and students in Sherryl's practicum to organize the conference. The grant included stipends of up to $175 for each of the S3! youth leaders who helped plan and colead the conference.

UNC afforded me the opportunity to create and teach COMM 89/53: Collective Leadership Models for Community Change, a service-learning course for first-year and transfer students. The course introduced students to communication activism approaches, then guided them in creating partnerships with youth-focused organizations, including the Ella Baker Women's Center's S3! group, to support positive community change projects. It was first taught in spring 2009, and I taught it each subsequent year through 2015. This is the course description from 2012:

Description

In this first-year seminar, we explore communication models for collective leadership involving youth and their allies in vulnerable communities. This is an APPLES service-learning course with a requirement of at least 30 approved hours of direct engagement with a designated community partner. Partnering with local youth-focused organizations, students will work in teams to research and design community-based change projects. Projects will focus on three key strategies that engage youth as leaders and stakeholders in communities: *youth media arts, youth organizing,* and *youth participatory action research.* Course readings, guest speakers, and class field trips will provide exemplars of successful work in these three areas as students work to create their own community-based projects. Students will write personal essays reflecting on their work in the class, engagement with the community, and participation at a public presentation of projects.

Class Trip: Final projects will be show cased or presented in poster sessions at a community-based venue with multiple stakeholders participating. This year, projects will be presented (as works in progress) at a student-led workshop at George Mason University, in Fairfax, VA, on **Friday and Saturday, March 30 and 31, 2012**, in partnership with Professor Arthur Romano and his students in the CON399 course on international peace education and conflict analysis. More details are forthcoming.

Sharing the Mantle Biennial Conference: In odd-numbered years, the projects are showcased or presented in poster sessions at the Sharing the Mantle youth leadership conference first convened as part of a special topics FYS in 2009 using Robertson Scholars funds. The Sharing the Mantle conference continues every two years in collaboration with Duke WISER (http://www.wisergirls.org/), this FYS, and the Ella Baker Women's Center for Leadership and Community Activism (http://ellabakerwomenscenter .org/). The conference brings together local activists working in youth empowerment and community change; student groups from UNC, Duke, and other area colleges and universities; and community groups engaging youth in collective leadership projects across traditional divides of culture, race, and economics. You are encouraged to attend and help produce the conference in 2013 as alumni of this FYS; see me for details.

With the exception of the 2012 field trip to George Mason University, the S3! student partner team always copresented their projects with senior youth leaders from the S3! cohort. Other student teams were required to demonstrate their commitment to centering youth voices in the cocreation and dissemination of knowledge in their respective teams, either at the conference or in some other venue. Six weeks of classroom training used the Kellogg Foundation's (2007) *The Collective Leadership Framework: A Workbook for Cultivating and Sustaining Community Change* and Boal's (2005) *Games for Actors and Non-Actors* to introduce students to the commitments underlying Ella Baker's belief in community power, group-centered leadership, and the use of critical pedagogies, to catalyze counter-storytelling communities in their work with youth. We also used Peter Block's (2008) *Community: The Structure of Belonging*, which provided other similar community-based models for collective organizing. Classroom training was followed by ten weeks of structured community work with three to four youth-serving organizations in addition to the Ella Baker Women's Center. However, from the beginning the course was geared to finding ways to engage the whole class in university-community collaborations or convenings, such as the preconference gathering in January 2009.

To orient the inaugural first-year seminar (FYS) students to community-engaged work, I sent out a call to the 2009 class a week before the course was set to begin, inviting them to a Sharing the Mantle preconference at the historically Black community center near Regal Gardens and University Heights. It was a longshot to get any students there, since some students had not even arrived on campus yet, but the two students who did attend, Reema Krais and Madhu Eluri, became the FYS-based students who teamed up with the S3! cohort. Indeed, the Saturday afternoon gathering had been co-organized by the senior S3! leaders, Chantel, Tania, Kennedy, and Jade, along with Duke student partners and the adult organizers of the CommUNITY Festival (Ms. Lynetta, Ms. Vergie, and Ms. Naomi). Naomi had borrowed a truck to bring the community mural created at the festival. Arthur's T.O. friends—Mikey, Rachel, and CJ—were on hand to lead the group through a series of T.O. activities that had the entire group moving through the space, sharing gifts, and affirming our desire to create a transformative conference that would catalyze intergenerational partnerships. For example, we began with a name game exercise that asked everyone to form a large circle to say each of their names while simultaneously performing a movement. In turn, the group would repeat each individual's name while performing that person's signature movement. There was a lot of laughter as the movements seemed to become bolder and more energetic. After that we did a "fill the space" exercise to continue building on the positive energy in the group. We ended the afternoon working in small groups to explore questions about challenges facing youth in underresourced communities and the role of adult allies in supporting youth activism. The intergenerational groups used image sculpting to reflect individual experiences in which they felt powerful and also situations in which they felt powerless to act against an injustice. From there, the groups generated some ideas about the root causes of challenges youth faced (such as the trend toward policing in schools). They recorded their responses on sticky notes, which were then placed on a large white board so that all the groups could survey them and discuss their reactions in a large circle during our closing session. We left the preconference with a wider network of allies and an affirmation from the S3! youth leaders that they were ready to coplan the first biennial Sharing the Mantle Conference working alongside Madhu and Reema from the UNC service-learning course (and another UNC student, Prasant Lokinendi).

One of the main purposes of the Sharing the Mantle Conference was to share our learning about developing youth-adult partnerships. One of the first steps in the planning process was to identify other community youth organizations that were already practicing aspects of youth-adult partnering aligned with one or more of the commitments that we were practicing: commitments to community power, group-centered leadership, and popular education to catalyze action. In the months leading up to the April 2009 Sharing the Mantle Conference, we engaged our social justice networks to find two groups that would serve as showcase groups alongside S3! One of those was a community-based group supporting girls becoming aware of their bodies and standards of beauty. Although they were not practicing group-centered leadership, we invited the group to attend one of our preplanning workshops and learn about the way S3! and their allies were learning social justice leadership. The adult leaders and youth participants were transformed by the experience and committed to working with our team to become one of the showcase groups at the conference.

Figure 6. S3! coplanning the 2009 Sharing the Mantle Conference. Photo by author.

The first biennial Sharing the Mantle Conference took place on April 17–18, 2019. Our collective of first-year UNC students (Reema, Madhu, and Prasant), S3! leaders (Chantel, Tania, Kennedy, Vanessa, Yvonne, and Jade) and adult allies (myself, Rachel, Arthur, CJ, and Mikey) designed the conference (see figure 6). The structure we created for the 2009 conference was sustained through subsequent conferences in 2011 and 2013. Each conference began with a kickoff on a Friday evening with dinner and a series of T.O. warm-up activities to orient the conference participants to our interactive format. The rest of the conference took place the next day (Saturday) from 9:00 a.m. to 4:00 p.m., with three "showcase" groups, including the S3! collective, leading interactive sessions on the conference theme. The 2009 theme was "Developing Youth/Adult Partnerships for Youth Leadership." The themes for the 2011 and 2013 conferences highlighted activities and learning in the context of "peace building" and "global connections." However, those conferences maintained the underlying focus on developing youth-adult partnerships for youth social justice leadership. That is, each Sharing the Mantle Conference sought these four outcomes for participants: gaining specific knowledge about developing, valuing, and sustaining youth and adult partnerships; learning strategies for building leadership capacity; learning strategies for productive youth-adult interactions; and creating networking opportunities for participants in attendance.

.   .   .   .   .

The rest of this chapter sketches four other projects from 2009 through 2013 that illustrate how our collective continued to create opportunities to exert community power and join other collaborators for broader social justice impact. Each of these projects began from or was advanced through S3!'s leadership and addresses an issue that was important to them. The cohort had grown to include one teen girl from a nearby neighborhood and three others within the neighborhood, including Jamilla, who had played a pivotal role in the CommUNITY Festival. The projects sketched in this section are the Harm Free Zones pilot project, the Raise the Age Campaign, the Comics Speak! project, and the Youth Bridging Cultures project.

A COUNTER-STORYTELLING COMMUNITY: HARM FREE ZONES, 2009–2010

> [The Director of Housing] is not happy with the overall reputation Regal Gardens currently has. [He/She] is working to fix this problem by having cops drive through the area during the night and to break up any formation of groups that are congregating outside.
> Undergraduate student research interview with College Town director of housing, 2009

The CommUNITY Festival became a mainstay in the neighborhood for five years. At the second annual event in October 2009, inspired by the theme "Celebrating What's Good in Our Neighborhood," Tawanna, Shana, and Crystal led (with two UNC students from the FYS) a series of community-building workshops. The workshops asked residents from Regal Gardens and University Heights to reflect on positive aspects of life in the community and challenges that got in the way of those positive aspects. They recorded summaries from the workshop on flip chart paper, and each group presented their summaries from the sound stage in the center of the park where the festival was happening. From those workshops a set of commitments emerged to focus on reducing conflict in the neighborhood, which residents believe often led to more negative police presence in the neighborhood. Out of that list was born a new partnership with the Durham, North Carolina–based SpiritHouse, which in turn launched a pilot of the Harm Free Zones project.

The Harm Free Zones project uses a restorative justice approach based on principles of community accountability intended to replace systems of state policing in communities. *Community accountability* refers to the ability and desire of community members to adopt a harm-free way of thinking. This includes developing the mechanisms to prevent harm, to intervene directly when harm occurs, to repair harm among community members, and to transform individual and collective relationships. Angela Davis, a longtime activist in the prison abolitionist movement, was one of the founding members of Critical Resistance, the organization that created the template for Harm Free Zones (Critical Resistance, 2018). The creation of Harm Free Zones is the historical process of building community autonomy and self-determination in the struggle to abolish the prison industrial complex and to transform our ways of treating each other, and it is inseparable from the process of community building.

When we encountered the project in the fall of 2009, it was being piloted in North Carolina neighborhoods and elsewhere around the United States. The Ella Baker Women's Center was invited by SpiritHouse to get training on how to implement the approach, and a few adult allies from the community started attending the meetings with me. They included Ms. Lynetta and Rachel Valentine, who had begun working as a program coordinator with the center. Lynetta seemed to take a special pride in playing a leadership role in this capacity. She often attended the Tuesday evening meetings in the city twenty minutes from her neighborhood in College Town after working long hours at her housekeeping job at a local hotel. Lynetta's involvement was an important part of the work.

Working with the girls was drawing in others from the community. As Ella Baker would say, "The tribe is growing."

After we completed the initial training, Regal Gardens/University Heights was selected as the site for a pilot test for the Harm Free Zones neighborhood approach.[5] This would involve a series of conversations in the neighborhood, led by the neighborhood group that had completed the training. The first meeting was held in September 2009 on a brisk, fall afternoon in the parking lot of the "D" building in Regal Gardens. Buildings were labeled "A," "B," "C," and "D" in descending order from the top of the hill ("up the hill") to the bottom. The residents of the "D" building in Regal Gardens referred to their area as the "D-Block" and prided themselves on being a close-knit group that looked out for each other. Residents from University Heights lived "up top," distinguishing them as spatially farther (and across a busy street) from those living in Regal Gardens "up the hill" from D-Block residents. Kennedy, Tania, Chantel, and Jade all lived in the D-Block. Kennedy (D-Block) and Jamilla (from up top) represented S3! at the meeting. Also in attendance at the first Harm Free Zones meeting, besides Lynetta and myself, were Arthur and four boys from the neighbor-hood—Antonio, Thomas, and Dante (all from the D-Block) and Chuckie from up top. There were no residents from up the hill.

Lynetta did a good job leading the conversation, standing before the group and asserting her role as leader. Jamilla wrote definitions and ques-tions on the flip chart and also joined in the conversation. Our questions were: "What is the Harm Free Zone?" (with key points taken from one of the handouts from our training) and "How can we come together so our kids can be safe?" (a question that came from the group after discussion). There was an intense conversation and some debate about the issues that led to harm in the community. Someone remarked that when conflict hap-pens, it is often started by people from outside the community who are visiting neighbors. Then the conversation turned to "agreements" that the D-Block has that help create a harm free zone. Lynetta explained that the D-Block sees itself as "family" and residents agree to look out for each other and commit to keeping everyone safe. She mentioned that folks up the hill will sometimes remark, "I want to live down in the D-Block."

Jamilla nodded her head in agreement with this and confirmed that she also had heard people say that before. That led us to the idea of having a "family reunion"–type street festival as a way to invite more participation and get people to share what they know about how to create safe spaces. So we left with the intention to return to that idea at the next Thursday's meeting.

After the initial meeting, the next step was to create personal invitations for each household to join us at the Thursday meetings. The following Monday, Ms. Jackie (Kennedy's mom) volunteered to organize with S3! members to create the invitations. The plan was to have more attendees from up the hill and up top. The event would be a potluck that would also include people from the larger collective of Harm Free Zones trainees from Durham. The goal would be to explore the question: "How can we come together so our kids can be safe?" and to get insights from D-Block "agreements."

A counter-story was boldly illustrated during that second Harm Free Zones meeting in the parking lot of the D-block. The police often come into the neighborhood, circling through, signifying that there is a presence of surveillance and control. As Lynetta led the conversation while Jamilla was taking notes on a flip chart, a police patrol car suddenly appeared, driving faster than it should down the hill. It slowed to a stop some distance away from the group and then slowly moved back up the hill in reverse. The group laughed and cheered at the sight of the police leaving the neighborhood in the face of this powerful gathering.

Significantly, over the next few months the Harm Free Zones group grew to engage in a parking lot summit at each of the sections of the neighborhood—up the hill and up top. The gatherings culminated with the family reunion–style festival coming to fruition. That celebration happened one sunny Saturday afternoon in July 2010; each family cooked out on their own stoop and joined together in the courtyard at the center to share food, fun, and fellowship. The Harm Free Zones celebration was an affirmation of the resolve to keep the neighborhood safe for the children. Lynetta declared later that fall, after the third annual CommUNITY Festival, that she could feel a noticeable difference in the way people in the two neighborhoods were supporting each other. To keep up the momentum, we sought more victories in our collective's new focus on restorative justice. The Raise the Age Campaign provided the next opportunity to pursue that goal.

FROM CONCEALED STORIES TO CRITICAL RESISTANCE: THE RAISE THE AGE CAMPAIGN, 2011–2013

In the summer of 2011, the S3! cohort was starting to get educated on a juvenile justice topic they'd heard about in 2009 at the youth activist mixer some of them had attended during our trip to Washington, DC (see chapter 3). At issue was the practice of locking up sixteen- and seventeen-year-olds with adult offenders, even if the youth had been charged with minor offenses. The practice was one of many that fueled the "school to prison pipeline" in North Carolina (Action for Children NC, 2013). Youth arrests often originated at high schools that were increasingly criminalizing student behaviors previously managed by school principals, counselors, and parents. Only two states had laws that allowed that practice: New York and North Carolina. We decided to travel to New York City to learn from youth activists there who were working on this issue.

S3! senior leaders Tania, Kennedy, Tawanna, and Shana made the trip (Vanessa wasn't able to go because of family obligations). Courtney McCluney, an Ella Baker Women's Center volunteer and recent UNC COMM Studies graduate, joined me as chaperone. Arthur, who was based in Brooklyn at that time, helped us make connections and plan our itinerary. Our first point of contact was youth justice advocate K. J. Rhee, director of the Center for Nu Leadership, housed at the time at Medgar Evers College in Brooklyn. K. J. provided us with workshop materials and flyers the staff at that center were using in their efforts to change New York's "stop and frisk" laws and raise the minimum age to eighteen when prosecuting adult offenders. K. J. gave us the names of three other groups, who invited us to come to their centers to meet with youth leaders and learn from them: Exalt Youth and the Center for Community Alternatives, two youth justice advocacy groups that create alternatives to incarceration programs with court-involved youth; and Sadie Nash, whose ELLA Fellowship program, named for Ella Baker, provides young women with social justice leadership training. The girls participated in roundtable conversations with youth activists at which they shared information about our work with the Harm Free Zones movement. We also did some sightseeing, including going to the places in Harlem and Greenwich Village where Ella Baker lived and did human rights work.

Back home, the girls were excited to share what they had learned with the rest of the cohort when our weekly Sunday afternoon leadership workshops resumed in August. Although the girls of S3! were just learning about the specifics of the laws and policies that helped fuel the school-to-prison pipeline, they were well aware of the trend toward policing in schools, including at their own high school, impacting their own neighborhood.

That fall, an arrest warrant was issued for Thomas on suspicion that he had stolen another student's cell phone while at school. The charges were eventually dropped, but not before the police had come to Regal Gardens after school one day looking for him. I happened to be with Naomi at a College Town visioning meeting (to help plan for the next decade of "excellence") when someone from the police department tipped her off that the police were looking for her son. We left the meeting to go search for Thomas. When we arrived in the parking lot near Naomi's apartment in the D-Block, there was no sign of the police. Then Thomas emerged from the woods behind Regal Gardens, where he had earlier fled. Visibly shaken and drenched in sweat, he got into my car, and Naomi called her friend at the police department to let them know that Thomas was coming to turn himself in. By that time it was dusk. When we arrived at the police station, the three of us got out of the car and walked toward the entrance. Two police officers emerged from the side of the building, and Thomas immediately dropped to his knees with his hands behind his back (he later told me his older brother had told him to do that if he were ever approached by the police in this kind of situation). I touched his shoulder and asked him to get up to stand between his mother and me, which he did. We cannot know if that spared Thomas the humiliation of lying face down on the grass with a knee in his back or some other act of violence, as sometimes happens in arrests of Black people, and sometimes in stark contrast with the experiences of White people being detained by police.[6] In any case, Thomas was handcuffed while standing up. His mother walked into the police station with him for processing, and he was released that same evening.

We were all outraged about what had happened to Thomas (even if the charges were eventually dropped). During our weekly meetings, the girls talked among themselves about the injustice of an arrest warrant being

issued at school for something as minor as a teen's missing cell phone, rais-
ing the prospect of youth being caught up in adult prison systems. The
following spring (2012), S3! was fully involved in the statewide campaign
to pass a law that would raise the age to eighteen as the minimum threshold for offenders sent to adult lock-up facilities in North Carolina, while
also calling attention to the injustices of school-based arrests for minor
offenses. In March, Kennedy and Tania joined me at a forum on the school-
to-prison pipeline that was hosted by the UNC Law School. There we met
Brandy Bynum Dawson from the child advocacy organization Action for
Children NC, which was spearheading the Raise the Age Campaign.[7] We
invited Ms. Bynum to come to the center to present a workshop on community outreach and mobilization, which Kennedy, Tania, Tawanna, and
Shana helped plan and facilitate. A new girl from a nearby neighborhood,
Lydia, also helped plan the forum and attended with her mother.[8]

The RTA workshop was well attended by parents and youth from
University Heights and Regal Gardens, including Thomas and others who
shared their experiences with the juvenile justice system. Ms. Bynum
thanked the group for sharing their stories and gave special recognition to
Kennedy, Tania, Tawanna, Shana, and Lydia for helping to organize the
community forum, which was an important part of the RTA grassroots
strategy. She also outlined the plans for S3! to get materials that would
guide them in engaging the "grass tops" aspects of the campaign: engaging the media, policy makers, and politicians on this issue. The grass tops
speaking-related activities became the main focus of our campaign efforts
for the rest of 2012 and into 2013. The girls did interviews on a local radio
show and presented at a Human Rights Week event at a senior citizen
community center and at an NAACP forum on UNC's campus. Lydia, then
sixteen, published an op-ed piece in the *College Town News* that sums up
S3!'s work on the RTA Campaign:

> The room was huge and flooded with college students. It was pretty dark,
> and as it got closer for me to speak, I could feel myself getting more nervous
> by the minute.
>
> I clutched my paper tighter as I felt my heart beating faster and faster.
> Suddenly it was my turn. "This is it," I whispered to myself as I made my way
> to center stage.

It had all started when I was introduced to a group called S3!, which stands for "Striving Sisters Speak!" I had met my group leader, Professor Patricia Parker, founder and director of the Ella Baker Women's Center, at an annual festival called "Neighborhood Night Out" held at the Hargraves Center in Chapel Hill.

She told us how she created the group to build leaders out of African-American [teen girls] like me to create positive change within and outside our communities. The group is based on the life's work of human rights activist, Ella Baker, who spent her childhood in Littleton, North Carolina and graduated valedictorian at Shaw University in 1927.

My mom and I decided to attend a meeting. When we got there, Professor Parker explained how every year we would learn about an issue, then plan and attend events to spread awareness. This is a part of her "learn, teach, lead" model—what she calls "critical pedagogy"—which empowers learners to teach others.

I knew that this was something I really wanted to do. My mother and I soon became very active in this group. It was not long before we started attending events about the "Raise the Age campaign" for 16- and 17-year-old youth offenders charged as adults, even when they are arrested for less serious or non-violent crimes. We even had the opportunity to talk with actual lawyers and judges about the injustice of the "school to prison pipeline."

We learned so much and worked so hard to promote awareness about this issue that I began to feel like a real activist!

Weeks later we knew that we were ready to present this information at a UNC showcase event. I was chosen to be a speaker for the presentation that we all prepared, which made me very nervous, considering that I tend to be very shy. But luckily I had the support of the S3! members, Professor Parker, and her students. They rehearsed with me several times, which really helped, especially since Professor Parker is an associate professor of communication studies at UNC–Chapel Hill.

When my turn finally came, I thought about everything Professor Parker had taught me. I looked all around the auditorium and could count about 100 people or more. I could see my mom and some of my S3! members sitting in the front middle row. Professor Parker was standing right beside me. The bright light was shining directly at me. Then I began to speak.

Afterward, I got some very supportive feedback and compliments, which really surprised me! I began to feel more confident and brave. All thanks to the group that started it all: S3!

But the best part of this is knowing that my group S3!, learned all of this together. We are like true sisters inside an intellectual and social journey that gives us the knowledge and confidence to let ourselves shine.
—Lydia

A bipartisan bill to raise the age of juvenile jurisdiction in North Carolina (H.B. 725) was finally passed in 2019, the last state in the nation to enact such a law (New York passed similar legislation in 2017). S3! was part of the efforts that made that happen. Lydia's essay is a reminder of the focus on "speaking our minds" that the founding S3! cohort saw as vital to social justice leadership.

The RTA Campaign marked the last S3! leadership project from Regal Gardens and University Heights. In 2013, the town made the decision to close the Family Resource Center that housed our collective's work. The Family Resource Center was a repurposed two-bedroom unit in the Regal Gardens complex. To help meet the demands for the growing need for affordable housing, College Town made the decision to reclaim the unit and rent it to a family waiting for housing. The Ella Baker Women's Center collective joined other community partners in lobbying the town to find alternative space for the center. Led by longtime community allies and some of the residents, we argued that the center was an important site for connecting the two neighborhoods and adding to the residents' sense of community. There was some initial rhetoric from town officials about possible spaces, but no action was ever taken to replace the center. By that time, everyone in the S3! cohort had graduated from high school and left the area, except for Lydia, who was in the tenth grade. All but two headed to college. Tawanna joined the Ella Baker Women's Center as a board member throughout her time in college and currently serves as secretary. I have maintained ties to the original cohort of leaders and their families.

The center relocated to Bonner Court Apartments, another of the thirteen public housing neighborhoods in College Town, which included a family resource center where we could share space. Delores Bailey, the bridge leader introduced in the introduction, connected us to families there. One teen from Regal Gardens made the trek over to Bonner Court, about two miles away. Seven other girls living in Bonner Court made up the 2013 S3! cohort. Their next two projects demonstrated S3!'s capacity for multiple ways of "speaking," including through visual arts and a return to T.O.

CREATING COUNTER-STORYTELLING ART: COMICS SPEAK! 2013

Comics Speak! was formed in response to a community need for expression, discussion, and collaboration. Funded by the College Town Public Arts Commission, the project was led by visual artist Luis Franco (Franco), spoken-word poet Kane Smego, and community organizers Amy Fischer (NC Dream Team) and me. The team's goal was to create a space for youth of color to use the arts to confront the obstacles they and their communities regularly encounter, as well as celebrate their vibrant cultural identities. The project provided space and instruction for Black, Latinx, and multiethnic youth to connect and to identify these issues, using both visual art and spoken word storytelling as a means for communicating among themselves and with the community at large. Lydia and two new girls (Mia and Nekia) represented S3! in the collective, along with Thomas and his cousin William. Thomas had participated in a poetry workshop that Kane had led at the center in Regal Gardens and was interested in continuing his learning, and he had invited his cousin. Kane had recruited two other Black high school students, one male and one female, whom he knew were excellent sketchers. Five Latinx high school students were involved in the movement to support the Deferred Action for Childhood Arrivals (DACA) program and related legislation. There were ten sessions. Five were writing workshops led by Kane, in which the youth could identify life experiences, cultural identities, and issues that they felt affected them. Franco taught the other five sessions, guiding the youth as they created illustrations that animated the images of their lives and identities that were developed in the writing workshops. Amy and I facilitated some parts of the sessions that used our expertise on collaborative youth engagement activities to build group solidarity.

At the first session, the youth decided to focus their stories on "superheroes" fighting social injustices in their communities, who would be graphically depicted in a comic book they would create. Working in small groups, the youth spent the ten weeks weaving together and illustrating their stories. The result was a collection of five short comics packed with powerful narratives and striking visuals. Their work was presented at three community events: a workshop led by the Comics Speak! youth at the 3rd Biennial Sharing the Mantle Conference; an art exhibit and spoken word performance at the local arts center in nearby Carrboro, North Carolina; and a book signing at a local comic store.

Kane Smego's vision of community-led collaboration provided the opportunity for the Ella Baker Women's Center and NC Dream Team to help secure the grant from the town. I was drawn to the project because I was interested in exploring how collaborative art making could be a mode of inquiry that brings into focus some of the complexities in organizing for social change and building coalitions. We found that indeed there were lessons to be learned when bringing together youth from different cultural/historical identities to do social justice work.

We used a decolonized approach to art making: artists who themselves were grounded in the community, art that was connected to questions from the community, and maintaining commitments to participatory knowledge production (knowledge from experts in the community guided the process alongside allies from outside the community). However, it was a challenge to create and sustain a process for the youth to speak their truths with each other and negotiate their activist identities when there was also pressure to create a product (the comic book, which had publishing deadlines). Black/biracial and Latinx youth come from different sociohistorical, gendered, and political standpoints. We needed to have a more consistent praxis to dialogue and reflect on what we were doing, including the complications of creating coalitions across divides. For example, when we juxtaposed a poem from a Latino youth honoring his hardworking father with one from a Black girl expressing her longing for a father she hardly knew, it needed to come with an analysis of the complex socioeconomic and historic structures that helped produce (and then deploy in political ways) both those poems.

So the challenge was having to balance between the process for the art to engage the youth in speaking their truths and the work it takes to make the product (a comic book). In the end, it was imperative for us to focus on producing the product because of our commitment to the grant. More time would have allowed us to do both more fully.

As in any community project, there were challenges just getting the same group of people in the room every week to create the work. Part of what we learned was the need to adapt to meet the needs of the community without losing site of the collective goals of the project. That kind of adaptive art making was better illustrated in the center's next project, Youth Bridging Cultures.

COACTIVE SPACES FOR STORYTELLING: YOUTH BRIDGING CULTURES PROJECT, 2013

Youth Bridging Cultures began as a partnership between the Ella Baker Women's Center and Michael (Mikey) Irwin, the English teacher at Chapel Hill High School who was among those who had first introduced S3! to T.O. systems. Irwin and I were both interested in deep learning about critical arts pedagogy in social justice work. In the summer of 2013, we devised a plan to unite students from the Scene & Heard Theatre Collective with students in my COMM 53 first-year seminar, scheduled for that fall semester. The Scene & Heard Collective was comprised of teachers and students from Chapel Hill High School dedicated to using personal and community stories to promote social justice. Mikey Irwin was the founder and adviser. The five Scene & Heard leaders and the fifteen COMM 53 students would join thirty local teens from different backgrounds for semester-long T.O. workshops that would culminate in a public performance at the local arts center. Through my networking with the Comics Speak! project, I had established connections with El Centro Hispano, NC, which engaged many of the Latinx teens from the NC Dream Team summer program. Thirteen El Centro students and their youth coordinator, Sandro Mendoza, joined the collective. Four S3! leaders joined the group, including Lydia and three girls from the new Ella Baker Women's Center site. Thirteen other youth joined—some from Irwin's school and others from Phoenix Academy, a local high school that was easily accessible from campus, which was the site of our collective's work.

For the first three weeks, Irwin came to my class to train the fifteen seminar students in T.O. methodologies (warm-up exercises and Image Theatre). They were also learning collective leadership models for entering communities, establishing trust, and creating coactive spaces for catalyzing social justice action. After that the students joined the five Scene & Heard leaders for one week of colearning and preparation for leading the twelve weeks of T.O. workshops.

The Youth Bridging Cultures collective included teens from different genders and ethnic identities: African American, White, Latinx, and Karen. Through the T.O. activities, they were able to use movement, language, sound, and visual art to explore various areas in their lives where they had dealt with structures of oppressive power—race, gender, nationalism—and how that often would produce conflict across differences.

After weeks of "radical rehearsal," and following Boal's principles of Forum Theatre (discussed previously in this chapter), the teens produced scenarios that were acted out in front of an engaged audience at the local arts center, where the Comics Speak! showcase had been staged. In Forum Theatre performances, audiences could stop the action at any moment to join the scene and act out a different outcome, resisting, exposing, or transforming the power structure. Discussion would follow.

In one particular scene, which included Alyssa, a member of S3!, the script called for Black girls arguing loudly in the school cafeteria and another Black girl whispering to her White friend that she was embarrassed by the spectacle. During the discussion period, a White woman from the audience asked Alyssa why the protagonist in the scene was loud and aggressive. Why choose that response in the first place? After a long silence, Alyssa responded, "Sometimes there is a need to be bigger—big gestures, loud words; it's something you learn." In the absence of a contextual analysis of the simultaneous hypervisibility and invisibility of Black women, "loudness" can be seen as a deficiency in need of correction. Alyssa spoke her truth of how a body learns to act otherwise out of necessity, and then, sometimes out of habit, a particular gesture remains. Standing beside Alyssa, affirming her truth, I shared in the forum my experience of making my way through historically White educational spaces, working through the tensions of being both hypervisible and invisible, and connecting my strategies for survival to the historical context that informed them.

.   .   .   .   .

Ella Baker's praxis for catalyzing leadership starts with commitments to community power (see chapter 2) and group-centered leadership (see chapter 3). But the eventual aim, as shown in this chapter, is to catalyze that leadership power in broader spheres of influence and in the process create counter-storytelling communities that expose the workings of oppression, such as racism, extreme capitalism, and militarism. Those systems were uncovered in the stories emerging from S3!'s coalitional projects, such as Harm Free Zones, Comics Speak!, and Youth Bridging Cultures. The lessons we learned along the way are woven into the stories told in this chapter. Collectively, those lessons relate to the joys and challenges of building meaningful relationships across lines of difference. It is hard work.

5 Rewriting Ella Baker's Daybook

INTEGRATING SELF-CARE AND ACTIVIST WORK

We who believe in freedom cannot rest.

Ella Baker (1964/2017)

Caring for myself is not self-indulgence, it is self-
preservation, and that is an act of political warfare.

Audre Lorde (2006)

The contents of Ella Baker's daybook during her time as a field secretary for the NAACP (1940–1943) reveal a relentless and difficult travel schedule.[1] She spent several months each year away from her home in Harlem, assisting branch leaders with membership drives, fundraising, and building local campaigns. Often she traveled alone throughout the Jim Crow South, typically by train or bus, where the unjust laws of segregation were sometimes enforced through harassment and violence. On at least two occasions she resisted demands to leave a section of a dining car when it was clearly within her rights to remain there. Baker's daybook also revealed an arduous itinerary of meetings and other engagements, at which she navigated constantly within patriarchal circles that questioned her belonging. From early September to late November 1941, she delivered sixty-three speeches in seven cities. In keeping with her developing philosophy, Baker also sought out as many opportunities as she could to create deeper connections with local people, sometimes spending as much as two weeks in a city touring the region and learning about local issues and concerns. In 1943, Baker was named director of branches, signifying the important and massive work she had done and would continue to do building up the NAACP's membership and catalyzing local people throughout the South to join the fight for freedom.

What was the emotional and psychological toll of all this? On the question of self-care, is Baker's life a cautionary tale, a source of inspiration, or some of both? This chapter presents fragments on radical self-care (Lorde, 2006) in the context of scholar-activism. The fragments are drawn from themes based on Baker's experience, my own experience, interviews and conversations with scholar-activists who have engaged in community work in the United States and transnationally, and historical and archival resources.

WE WHO BELIEVE IN FREEDOM CANNOT REST?

It is not unusual for Black women social change agents to view Ella Baker's schedule as normal and to have a moment of recognition when they see her daybook. At the SNCC fortieth anniversary celebration, veteran activist Muriel Tillinghast said, "Ms. Baker's diary reads like an itinerant back roads preacher in the '40s, which is in many ways how we functioned."[2] The diary resonates with twenty-first-century activists as well. Cynthia Brown, an activist and member of the Greensboro, North Carolina, Truth and Reconciliation Commission, told me in July 2013, "When I read Barbara Ransby's biography of Ella Baker, I said to myself, now what I'm doing makes sense. It was the first time I saw myself—what I was doing—modeled in someone else's life's work."

Coumba Touré, one of the coordinators of the organization Africans Rising, had the same self-recognition: "When I discovered Ms. Baker in the 1990s through *Ella's Song*, I thought, 'That's me! That is the work I do!'" (personal communication, June 2018). Bernice Johnson Reagon, a founding member of SNCC and later of the group Sweet Honey in the Rock, wrote *Ella's Song* using the words of wisdom her mentor had spoken over the years. This is the refrain, quoted at the beginning of this chapter:

We who believe in freedom cannot rest
We who believe in freedom cannot rest until it comes.

I do not know Ms. Baker's intent in these words with regard to self-care. I can only say that I understand the urgency of the context in which she spoke them, typified by this stanza in *Ella's Song*:

> Until the killing of Black men, Black mothers' sons
> Is as important as the killing of White men, White mothers' sons
> We who believe in freedom cannot rest until it comes.

I believe, as Ella Baker did, that as long as injustice continues, the struggle for justice must also. The struggle continues until the systems that feed on White supremacy and patriarchy are dismantled. Oppressive power continues to rearticulate itself into new arrangements. It will not stop on its own.

> Until the . . .
> > Violence against Black trans women,
> > > cis women, gender non conforming, queer, and trans-non-binary
> > folks,
> > Annihilation of indigenous people,
> > Separation of immigrants and their children at borders,
> > Mass incarceration in for-profit prisons,
> > Destruction of the planet,
> >
> > . . .
> >
> > Can be halted.
> > We who believe in freedom *dare* not rest.

.   .   .   .   .

The everyday struggle for social justice is *exhausting*. This word recurs often in people's accounts of activism, including my own, as I share later.[3] There is an emotional toll that comes from confronting White supremacy. A statement from a convening in greater Manchester, England, organized by the Trafford Rape Crisis center on its fifth anniversary, captures this sentiment: "The effects of racism and sexism, mixed up with other pressures such as poverty, disability and homophobia, [are] exhausting" (Nayak, 2015, p. 8). Historian Russell Rickford, who has studied the Black Lives Matter (BLM) movement, has noted, "Demanding accountability for racist violence and an immediate end to the murder of black people at the hands of the state, . . . their mainstay has been occupation—

of highways, intersections, sporting events, retail stores, malls, campaign events, police stations, and municipal buildings. They have organized 'die-ins,' marches, and rallies in multiple cities, viewing creative disturbance as a means of dramatizing routine attacks on black life" (Rickford, 2016, p. 36). Direct action tactics are emotionally and physically exhausting and can take their toll.

I am at the Southern Jam at Highlander Research and Education Center in August 2017. Two women activists from the BLM movement are among the participants. We listen to and hold their stories of the emotional toll that comes with being on the frontlines of the movement, where they have both worked as organizers. They are at Highlander for support, reflection, and a plan for revival. One of them has brought Adrienne Maree Brown's (2017) new book, *Emergent Strategy*, to share with the group. A quote from Ella Baker prefaces the contents for readers: "This may only be a dream of mine, but I think it can be made real." It is a book filled with hopeful strategies that embrace the complexity of the freedom struggle and the promise that we are enough to make the dream real. Brown has been influenced by Grace Lee Boggs, who walked and worked with Ella Baker. She was also influenced by Octavia E. Butler (2012), the award-winning science fiction writer whose work, like the *Parable of the Sower*, inspires imaginative movement work, and Margaret J. Wheatley (1994), who wrote the foundational text on emergence theories in leadership. For Brown, the clearest articulation of the concept of emergence comes from Nick Obolensky: "Emergence is the way complex systems and patterns arise out of a multiplicity of relatively simple interactions" (2017, quoted on p. 2). Drawing on the wisdom of Butler, Brown has asked, "How can we, future ancestors, align ourselves with the most resilient practices of emergence as a species?" (2017, p. 14).

I think one implication of Brown's thesis is that Ella Baker's approach embraces that complexity: all the paradoxes and contradictions (some activists have spoken of invigorating exhaustion); the whole as a mirror of the parts. Staying in the struggle is a necessity for changing systems of injustice. But resting does not have to mean quitting. Resting can be a path to freedom.

.   .   .   .   .

In December 2019, I'm in Rio de Janeiro, Brazil. During a break from my studies and training at the Center for the Theatre of the Oppressed, I'm giving a talk about Ella Baker to a group of Black feminists. Two other participants, Philadelphia-based artists Shanel Edwards and Ashley Davis, are copresenters. They open the talk with a performance. Shanel, a Black queer nonbinary dancer, photographer, and poet in their twenties, delivers a powerful interpretive dance with *Ella's Song* playing in the background. Their movement echoes the pain of being in the struggle for freedom. Freedom is breaking through with every movement as well. Our host and translator, Dr. Joselina da Silva, has distributed to the thirty or so participants the words to *Ella's Song* in Portuguese. Poet Ashley Davis's work has been described as "fearless work that can be equal parts devastating and liberating." Ashley joins the performance with a poem, riffing on Ella Baker's words:

Who?
Who?
Who believes in freedom? Who believes in freedom?
Who believes in freedom? Who believes in freedom?
Who believes in freedom? Who believes in freedom?
Who believes?

We believe. We believe in freedom. We who believe?
We who believe in freedom! We who believe in freedom!
We who believe in freedom!
We who believe in freedom cannot rest.
We who believe cannot rest! We who believe cannot rest!
We who believe, we cannot rest. We cannot rest.

We who believe in freedom cannot rest until it comes.
We who believe in freedom cannot rest until it comes!
We who believe in freedom cannot rest until it comes.
We who believe in freedom cannot rest until it comes.

We who believe cannot rest. We who believe cannot rest. We who believe
cannot rest.

We cannot rest. We cannot rest. We cannot rest.

We cannot rest! We cannot rest.
We cannot rest! We cannot rest.
We cannot rest. We cannot rest!

We cannot rest? We cannot rest.
Cannot rest?
Cannot rest?
Cannot rest. Cannot rest. Cannot rest. Cannot rest. Cannot rest. Cannot rest.
    Cannot rest. Cannot rest, cannot! Cannot rest!
Cannot rest? Cannot rest? Cannot rest?
Cannot rest? Cannot rest? Cannot rest?
Rest! Rest! Rest! Rest! [Bows to each person in the room.]
Rest. Rest. Rest. Rest. Rest. Rest.

Rest.
Rest.
. . . Rest . . .
. . . Rest . . .
Rest. Rest.
Rest! Rest!
Rest? Rest? Rest.
Rest! Rest! Rest!
Rest? Rest. Rest. Rest . . . rest . . . rest . . . rest . . . rest . . . rest . . .
We believe?
We believe freedom is rest.
We believe, we believe freedom is rest.
We believe freedom is rest.

As Dr. da Silva translates, Ashley engages the audience in a call and response. The performance seems to resonate with the women, as some of them call back, "I believe in freedom!" Ashley engages Shanel as well, in turns, signifying through rapid movement—up, down, up, down—to the beat of Ashley's cadence: cannot rest, cannot rest, cannot rest. The performance ends as Ashley connects with each person via eye contact as she moves about the room, gesturing with outstretched arms, palms open, bowing, blessing each one: rest, rest . . . as Shanel and Ashley slowly release themselves to the floor, at rest. Rest is a pathway to freedom. Each of us must find our own path to radical self-care if we are to stay in the struggle.

SELF-CARE IS AN ACT OF POLITICAL WARFARE

Like Baker's call to those who believe in freedom, Audre Lorde's words, quoted at the beginning of this chapter, also beckon us to stay in the struggle. She penned those words as she was battling cancer, at times visualizing the cancer as "the face and shape of my most implacable enemies, those I fight and resist most fiercely" (2006, p. 133). She writes, "Visualizing the disease process inside my body in political images is not a quixotic dream. When I speak out against the cynical US intervention in Central America, I am working to save my life in every sense. Government research grants to the National Cancer Institute were cut in 1986 by the exact amount illegally turned over to the contras in Nicaragua. One hundred and five million dollars" (p. 133). Audre Lorde reminds us that the personal is the political.

Angela Davis's vision applies here as well. She wrote that "the pursuit of health in body, mind and spirit weaves in and out of every major struggle women have ever waged in our quest for social, economic and political emancipation" (1984/1990, p. 54). If we are to understand self-care as a condition for staying in the struggle, we must ask: What do we need to be fully present and accountable to ourselves and to our communities (see Scott, 2016)? Ella Baker kept a relentless schedule, but she also had a deep well of personal integrity and experienced deep and sustaining connections with other activists and community members. In my own practice and in talking with other activists who have been intentional about self-care, these two dimensions—personal integrity and sustaining connections—are foundations of radical self-care in social justice activism.

I have come to understand self-care as, ultimately, care for the spirit of self and others. In that sense, what would a *daily practice* of self-care involve? In 2011, I participated in a weeklong Theatre of the Oppressed workshop for educators. I was exhausted going into the workshop. As recounted in this book, for four years I had poured my heart into the emotional, intellectual, psychological, and physical labor of being in community with people across raced, classed, gendered, generational, and spatial boundaries. From 2007 to 2013, my community-engaged work consisted of organizing with the girls, my students, community activists, and other collaborators. I had created and still served as executive director of the Ella Baker Women's Center. In addition, I had created a first-year seminar (see chapter 4) to train undergraduate students during the regular academic year as they learned community-based collective leadership. During the summers, I had served as a full-time mentor to pregraduate students learning the same. All the while, I had attended to my other duties as a professor at a research I university—a Black woman navigating the racialized and gendered spaces of a historically White southern institution. It was exhausting.

This is what it feels like to try to "hold back the ocean with a broom" (Gilkes, 1980), as one activist has described Black women's community work. The Theatre of the Oppressed workshop I participated in during late July 2011 freed the ocean. Instead of drowning, I felt a release. From the very first activity there seemed to be a shift in my spirit. We were partnered with another participant and then, with one partner's eyes closed, the other was released into a mix of a dozen other participants, walking through the space listening for your partner's gentle calling of your name.

"Can you discern your name from among the others?" is what the facilitator said. What I heard instead was, "What is *your* calling in the work of social justice?"

Later that week, when we performed the Forum Theatre, a woman in the audience reacted to my scene, in which I played a Black woman responding frantically to all the stereotypical images of her—Sapphire, Mammy, Black-Lady-Over Achiever. She said, "I don't hear *your* desires. What do you desire?" It was as if something shifted in my very being. To take seriously my own desires seemed radical in that moment. My life changed.

I began to seek my innermost thoughts through audio journaling. It was a dialogue with the divine, like Alice Walker's Celie in *The Color Purple*. The dialogue was productive and healing, excavating dark places, affirming all that is good. I discovered Lorde's (1978) essay "Uses of the Erotic: The Erotic as Power" and understood its connection to divine sustaining energy as a form of radical self-care. Lorde wrote: "The very word *erotic* comes from the Greek word *eros*, the personification of love in all its aspects—born of Chaos, and personifying creative power and harmony. When I speak of the erotic, then, I speak of it as an assertion of the life-force of women; of that creative energy empowered, the knowledge and use of which we are now reclaiming in our language, our history, our dancing, our loving, our work, our lives" (1978, p. 56).

I now have more than four hundred audio journal recordings filling three digital recorders. This daily practice has become routine: positive self-talk that affirms my right to be free from self-doubt and fear but also affirming my need for connection to others, especially those with whom there is a conflict. As part of my daily practice, I listen to some of the earlier recordings, annotating synchronous themes and resonances in a written journal that guides me toward stronger connections among a community of activists, allies, and family members. I have come to see the most challenging relationships as part of a perfecting process in my own journey toward humanity. Social justice work for me is a perfecting process that begins in one's own life and extends to others.

INTEGRATING SELF-CARE AND ACTIVISM

Activists committed to being accountable to people in communities need the support of safe spaces throughout their time as activists, not just in times when they take respite after getting exhausted. For some scholar-activists, building community relationships provides a space away from toxic environments that sometimes characterize bureaucratic institutions. I feel fortunate that in the past eight years or so, in addition to the relationships I developed through the Ella Baker Women's Center, I have discovered a growing number of spaces for activists to gather—to restore, recharge, and reactivate as needed. Highlander has always been that place. Others I have discovered are Yes! Jams, based in Oakland, which also happen across the globe. A proliferation of such spaces is needed in communities as well as within the institutions that engage them. These are the kinds of "free spaces" Ella Baker called for (see chapter 1). The integrative work that happens within such spaces catalyzes attention to the care of the body, mind, and spirit.

. . . . .

Sasheer Zamata is a former cast member of *Saturday Night Live*. In a story for *This American Life* on NPR, she interviewed her mother, Ivory, who by herself desegregated the White school in rural Forrest City, Arkansas. She spoke of the taunts and violence she experienced. But what she remembered most was feeling alone and abandoned. Sasheer seemed to be hearing the story for the first time and was amazed that her mother did not see herself as a civil rights hero. At the same time that Sasheer's mother was on the frontlines of antiracist work in Forrest City, the Little Rock Nine (which the teenaged Ivory read about in *Ebony*) were being supported and mentored by Dorothy Height. She had no one to provide the support of a relational structure and the historical analysis for her to see the fierceness of her own power. Ella Baker provided that kind of space for the groups she supported. The work I have attempted to do with the Ella Baker Women's Center is in that tradition as well. I hope this book becomes an affirmation for others doing the same and an inspiration to those who desire to follow that path.

Conclusion

In the current context, characterized by threats to democracy across the globe, masses of ordinary people—especially youth—are heeding the call for civic activism, through platforms such as social media campaigns, public protests, and community-based organizing (Dutta, 2011; Ransby, 2018; Velasquez & LaRose, 2015). In the United States, activism is being driven by the persistence of state-supported terror against Black lives; the racist, xenophobic, and misogynist policies of the Trump administration; and an unchecked gun culture that fuels community violence and mass killings at schools (Edwards-Levy, 2017; Galston, 2018; Liu, 2017). For example, the youth-led Black Lives Matter movement, a network of over fifty organizations as of 2017, was sparked by outrage over the 2012 vigilante murder of Trayvon Martin and the exoneration of his killer, then accelerated during the Ferguson, Missouri, uprising after the police shooting of Michael Brown Jr. in his neighborhood (Ransby, 2018).[1] For decades the United States has been characterized by what Hartnett aptly termed a "punishing democracy," in which violence persists at the heart of the American experience (2011, p. 6). In the United States as well as globally, neofascism is on the rise, and the deep structural causes of economic suffering among the working and middle classes persist (Inglehart &

Norris, 2016). Now, perhaps more than ever, there is an urgent need to apply Ella Baker's community power–driven philosophy and praxis for social justice leadership.

The case study presented in this book translates into one community in which Baker's group-centered praxis was applied as a catalytic leadership approach. It responds to a need for social justice leadership communication processes that *catalyze* personal routes to collective consciousness about social justice and *mobilize* collective action in interorganizational collaborations. In focusing on working *with* people in communities, Baker's praxis resembles Gramsci's understanding of subalternity and common sense/*bueno senso* as a method of tapping into and engaging local knowledge toward emancipatory practices. Baker directs attention to deep and persistent *structural analyses* of power along with mechanisms to support *individual routes to collective action*. Her praxis is also intersectional. Intersectionality, as defined by Collins and Bilge (2016), is most useful as an analytical tool—a heuristic that can be used to understand domains of power and global inequality. In other words, any neighborhood or community will contain people who are situated within a multiplicity of power relations that are mutually constituted and reinforcing. However, Baker calculated that there are people living under the heels of injustice who have done the structural analysis and have a keen understanding of the workings of power. They are often laboring alone to educate others about what is happening in the here and now, perhaps without the resources to build movements or to scale up action. Baker was adept at uniting with various community-based activists who identified with others according to race, class, gender, or age and connecting them with resources. She communicated in ways that built within- and across-group solidarity and then helped people make connections to urgent questions about state power and collective routes to democracy for all (Ransby, 2003).

Now, as then, that kind of intersectionality and connection building is a necessary strategy for fueling social justice action and structural change. As a social movement strategy, an intersectional approach flourishes in what Baker referred to as "free spaces," where people have access to a structural analysis of power drawn from their *own* experiences and can also "envision and enact new social relations grounded in multiple axes of intersecting, situated knowledge" (Chun et al., 2013, p. 917). Baker conceptualized community power as individual accountability to collective action. And that kind of power has to be built over time.

·   ·   ·   ·   ·

Ella Baker understood that people from all walks of life have different motivations to engage in social justice organizing and activism. With her staunch belief in democracy for all, she promoted strategies that could open pathways for civic engagement for anyone, regardless of motivation. Her belief and strategy involved engaging with the hidden transcripts of people's everyday experience with systemic (local, state, global) violence and oppression (J. C. Scott, 1990). "Hidden transcripts" are the concealed stories of everyday life that build up a cache of wisdom in a community about resisting the status quo. This kind of engagement, she believed, could catalyze *individual routes toward collective action* and advance social justice leadership for a radical, plural democracy.

In the early twenty-first-century context, however, some of the most common routes toward collective action for social justice for people in vulnerable communities run through the complicated context of organizational-community collaborations, such as my role as a university-affiliated director of a community-based organization. There are many organizations populated by everyday people who become influencers of policies, customs, and laws. Civil society organizations are also known as the rapidly growing "third sector" (Anheier, 2014). Strictly speaking, third-sector organizations are neither government nor public administration agencies (the first sector), nor are they the for-profit corporate entities of business and commerce (the second sector). Organizations in the third sector are nonprofits and NGOs, which represent "the sum of private, voluntary, nonprofit organizations, and associations," hereafter referred to as nonprofits (Anheier, 2014, p. 4).[2] Nonprofits encompass a diverse array of institutions, organizations, and activities, ranging from entities such as a local daycare for children to elite universities such as Harvard, Yale, or Stanford, which have become billion-dollar nonprofit corporations; labor unions; and humanitarian relief associations and international development organizations, such as Doctors Without Borders. Nonprofits are sometimes attached to first- and second-sector organizations, as in the case of corporate philanthropy or government-run aid agencies, and they are prominent on virtually every continent. In the United States, nonprofit organizations had a $14.5 trillion share of the gross domestic product in 2010 (Roeger et al., 2012, p. 22, reported in Anheier, 2014, p. 106).

Nonprofits tend to have a strong ideological attachment to empowerment projects and ambiguous influences on the spaces and economies where they operate, so they are situated paradoxically as forces for both good and harm in their partnerships with community residents. Many nonprofit organizations have the stated or implied intention to enlist volunteers and paid staff to help solve the world's pressing problems (Eliasoph, 2013). Paradoxically, however, the very resources intended to support communities and solve problems often become tools for oppression and sources of larger problems. As Eliasoph (2013) has illustrated clearly, organization-community "partnerships" have resulted in many harmful outcomes. Among other things, they have undermined local communities' own efforts to achieve transparency, self-determination, and sovereignty; proliferated neoliberal "empowerment projects" that rely on "blame the victim" approaches; jeopardized local economies; and sometimes created power inequalities that pit neighbors against each other (pp. 94–128).

The paradoxes of institutional support in organizational-community interventions, for example, are captured forcefully in Cole's (2012) account of the "White-savior industrial complex" as it applies to NGOs operating in Africa. Cole was responding (via tweets and in longer form) to the global phenomenon *Kony 2012*, a thirty-minute video developed by a White filmmaker, Jason Russell, for the NGO Invisible Children, Inc. The video's stated intention was to bring attention to Joseph Kony, an indicted war criminal in Uganda, in hopes that he would be arrested before the end of 2012. The video went viral on YouTube, with millions of views, and was especially taken up by young American adults (Rainie et al., 2012). Cole saw this as a prime example of the White-savior industrial complex, in which someone "from America or Europe can go to Africa and become a godlike savior or, at the very least, have his or her emotional needs satisfied . . . under the banner of 'making a difference' . . . while ignoring the 'intricate and intensely local problems' that communities are already engaging" (2012, n.p.). Cole argued that the complex is structured to ignore policies that Whites have created and that maintain systems of oppression.

Similarly, academics at elite universities (and other civil society organizations) attempting to do community-based organizing are sometimes advancing the neoliberal logics of state power. The paradoxical "collusions and complicities between state and civil society, specifically youth activist nonprofit organizations . . . together mediate and manage youth as political actors and democratic subjects" (Kwon, 2013, p. 5). That is, organization-community partnerships are often advancing oppressive power in communities even as they purport to advance community "empowerment" (Eliasoph, 2013).

Scholar-activists aim to avoid the problems of collusion and complicity between state and civil society through a commitment to changing the status quo to support social justice for all. They understand activist scholarship as "active engagement between the academy and movements for social justice" and a commitment to plural, participatory democracy (Sudbury & Okazawa-Rey, 2009, p. 3). From this perspective, when scholar-activists and others committed to plural, participatory democracy enter into organization-community partnerships, they need to be mindful of the kind of bounded spaces they create through their interactions (Dempsey, 2007). Engagement needs to be oriented toward the creation of spaces and support for agonistic dialogue (Mouffe, 2000). Agonisms become a sign of a healthy democracy, a container for oppositional thinking in which the boundaries are drawn by a commitment to plural, participatory democracy (Golding, 1992).

In my view, this call for agonistic dialogue suggests an urgent role for university-community collaborations to advance social justice. Although universities are situated uniquely and, in the US context, missioned historically to advance civic engagement (Geiger, 2014), there are unsettled debates about the notion of "civic engagement" locally and globally, the role of these institutions as community partners in such engagement, and the necessary capacities to sustain university-community partnerships for social justice activism (Gardinier, 2017; Hardy et al., 2003). Indeed, there is the ever-present potential for glossing over power differentials in university-community partnerships, since institutional actors always have the most powerful roles, but this sociopolitical power itself can easily be erased and deconstructed within the discourse of civic engagement. Capacities for collaboration are necessary but not sufficient for social justice leadership to mobilize action, particularly when people in vulnerable communities are involved.

To understand university-community collaborations in the United States and globally, we must take into account the persistent hierarchical structuring of relations built on legacies of extreme capitalism, colonialism, institutionalized slavery, and White supremacy (Collins, 1990; Parker et al., 2018; Giovanni, 1994). As I write this conclusion, universities across the United States (not just the southern regions) are being forced to confront the meaning of monuments celebrating the Confederacy—and the legacy of anti-Black racism they were meant to advance—that for over a century have occupied campus landscapes in the form of statues, buildings, and other memorials. These symbolic gestures in support of racism continue to exist on historically White campuses. The very real impacts of institutionalized racism persist as well, in the form of racial and gender inequities in access to education, hiring practices, promotions, salaries, and so on.

These conditions have urgent and often toxic implications for university-community collaborations. Indeed, many universities in the United States, whose stated missions are to advance the public good, are situated paradoxically within areas of persistent poverty, where local people experience overpolicing, immigration abuses, and inadequate housing. These conditions, furthermore, are traceable to contemporary university policies and practices, over which the community has little or no meaningful control (see, e.g., Eliasoph, 2013; Gardinier, 2017). Globally, as universities increasingly engage with corporate partners to find innovative solutions to community-based problems, people at "the margins of contemporary societies . . . are systematically erased from dominant discursive spaces of knowledge production" (Dutta, 2011, pp. 2–3).

Universities increasingly are calling for and supporting community engagement to ameliorate social justice inequities (Barinaga & Parker, 2013).[3] Accordingly, students, faculty, and administrators need to be prepared, intellectually and practically, to take into account the complexities of organizational-community collaborations. In writing this book, I join scholars from across disciplines who have called for decolonizing analyses of the academy (see Davies et al., 2003, for a review). For decades these scholars have made the case that analyzing the racist past and legacies of slavery in the eighteenth and nineteenth centuries is the interpretive key to creating futures that are more inclusive and accessible for everyone, and this is part of what they mean by decolonizing practices. Ahmed (2012) has argued that advancing diversity initiatives without a decolonizing critique risks reproducing racist and White supremacist structures of relations.

Ella Baker's catalytic leadership approach engages in critical, antiracist, and socially just community engagement according to a decolonizing principle. Her organizing approach embeds a leadership communication process—a learn-teach-lead method—that catalyzes *personal* routes to *collective* consciousness and provides a framework for collective leadership action. Relational theories of leadership communication tend to emphasize individual goal setting and leader-member exchanges without considering routes to collective leadership (see Northouse, 2016). Other theories, such as servant leadership, start with the premise that people are born with a desire to serve others (Greenleaf, 1977). In contrast, Baker's group-centered philosophy of praxis emphasizes a participative form of organizing that catalyzes strategic and tactical communication (see Poletta, 2005). Her praxis begins with an analysis and articulation of how people come to *learn* how oppressive power operates in their everyday lives and how to work with others to build their capacities to intervene in those problems. Then it considers how people can *teach* what they have learned to others and ultimately how they can further build their capacities by *leading* social justice actions (Grant, 1998; Payne, 1995/2007; Ransby, 2003). Baker's signature workshop series, developed in the 1940s, was called Give Light and People Will Find the Way. It was her way of catalyzing leadership in communities of the Jim Crow South (Grant, 1998). It exemplifies her philosophy of what I call *catalytic social justice leadership.*

Catalytic social justice leadership develops through actual practice in the midst of struggle. It is both *knowledge producing* and *relational.* As a knowledge-production process, catalytic social justice leadership is grounded in practices that nurture group process, such as critique, problem solving, collaboration, and persuasion. Validity, what counts as knowledge, is understood as "the degree to which the research process reorients, focuses, and energizes participants toward knowing [a] reality in order to transform it" (Lather, 1986, p. 272).

Ella Baker understood that a critical analysis of how state and corporate power circulates to create violence and inequity is accessible in the concealed stories of those who live under those actual conditions. When their stories are shared within the context of organizing for social justice, they can ignite collective consciousness and aid in the transformation of society toward social justice. Storytelling can be the foundation for a kind of intrinsic motivation that forges individual routes to collective consciousness. Baker's approach is about coming to consciousness about how individual experience and practice connects to a collective effort to create a democratic society.

Popular movement narratives seldom discuss these relational processes and political praxis that organize masses of people living in the oppressive conditions of capitalism. A theory of social justice leadership, grounded in a vision of radical democracy and participative practice, must take into account the political, social, and material complexities embedded within individual identities (Foucault's [1977] "technologies of the self"). Catalytic organizing for social justice is also a relational process that imagines multiple personal routes to collective consciousness and holds in productive tension messy, contradictory, and paradoxical relational dynamics that emerge across lines of difference between people based on race, class, gender, age, and religion. Validity in this context means communication principles and practices that create participative spaces in which people—both allies from outside organizations and people in vulnerable communities—can see themselves as experts and employ that expertise to promote social justice.

Throughout this book, knowledge production and relational dynamics have been revealed as the foundations for *collective leadership* in Baker's praxis. It is a social learning process that adheres to specific participative commitments and practices that attend to both individual and relational contexts. It is important *not* to treat the commitments presented in this case study in a linear fashion. Rather, recognizing that antiracist social justice organizing is dynamic, there is a need for collectives to sometimes start over or sprint to a moment of catalyzing impact, depending on the efficacy of the group's commitments to those actions. Ella Baker's approach is about integrating these commitments as everyday praxis. It illustrates the many and various entry points for catalyzing social justice leadership in organizational-community partnerships. The struggle continues. Someone else carries on.

APPENDIX 1   Case Study Timeline

Chapter 2. "People Under the Heels of Oppression Should Be the Ones Leading": Entering into Community Partnerships

February 2003–July 2006	Bridge leaders/administrators at the Family Resource Center at Regal Gardens and University Heights connect with Parker via St. Paul AME Church to organize events involving parents and young children in the neighborhood, including "mother-daughter" picnics to share stories of mother wisdom over catered lunches.
	Conducts qualitative interviews with community experts as preparation for entering community collaboration
August 2006–May 2007	UNC research and study leave/Kauffman Foundation–funded fellowship provides Parker with resources to incorporate the Ella Baker Women's Center for Leadership and Community Activism as a not-for-profit organization.
	Networking with Innovation Center and Kellogg Foundation fellows
	Parker volunteers as tutor at Family Resource Center, lingers in the neighborhood to talk with parents and youth.
	Strowd Roses Grant: Receives $10K, which allows a course release for fall 2007 to mentor graduate students and work alongside youth teams in the coming year
	IRB approval for the Still Lifting, Still Climbing research project

Chapter 3: "Think in Radical Terms": Creating Participative Spaces for Social Justice Organizing

June 2007	Still Lifting, Still Climbing project kickoff
	S3! is formed by seven teen girls.
	Summer workshops inspired by Ella Baker's philosophy of community power; KLCC Framework (Build Trust, Co-Construct Purpose, Act Together, Sustain); and Innovation Center's Youth/Adult Partnership Learning and Leading tool kit.
August 2007	Visioning retreat
September 2007–March 2008	Dumpster Project
March 2008	Trip to Boston; S3! redirects collective focus on a CommUNITY Festival to support youth in the neighborhood
April–September 2008	Learn-Teach-Lead workshops emerge around festival planning.
October 2008	First Annual CommUNITY Festival

Chapter 4: "Strong People Don't Need Strong Leaders": Engaging Social Justice Storytelling for Catalytic Leadership

October 2008	Presentation at Judith Blau's sociology class on social movements; participation in Human Rights Month activities
	Robertson Grant Award to support research partnership of UNC–Chapel Hill, the Ella Baker Women's Center, and Duke University
	One condition of this research grant is for the students to present their findings at a conference. Writing this grant inspires the creation of Parker's **first-year seminar**, which supports S3! and other community partners in hosting the first biennial **Sharing the Mantle Conference** on youth/adult partnerships in social justice organizing.
	S3! senior leaders and the Robertson Grant team start planning the Sharing the Mantle Conference.
November 2008	S3! hosts an election-night watch party.
January 2009	**January 7:** Sharing the Mantle preconference at the historically Black community center brings together students from Parker's first-year service-learning course, five S3! leaders, and youth and adult organizers of the CommUNITY Festival (Lynetta, Vergie, Naomi, Moni, Antonio, Thomas, Jamilla). Naomi has borrowed a truck to bring the community mural created at the festival. Two incoming first-year UNC students, Reema Krais and Madhu Eluri, join the collective, although classes will not start until a week later.

January 12: S3! speaks at a town council meeting about representing College Town at the inauguration of the first Black president of the United States.

January 16–21: S3! senior leaders Vanessa, Jade, Chantel, Tania, and Kennedy attend President Barack Obama's inauguration, along with adult allies Pat, Lynetta, Dorita, Alyssa, and Stacey. S3! is one of four youth groups selected nationally by the Stafford Foundation to attend its "People's Inauguration."

Stacey and Alyssa accompany the girls to the youth social justice networking night during the People's Inauguration, where they first learn about the juvenile justice efforts in New York to change laws about locking up sixteen- and seventeen-year-olds in adult detention centers and prisons.

February–March 2009	COMM 89/53, Collective Leadership Models for Social Change, is launched and underway with fifteen students partnering with community-based youth-focused organizations, including the Ella Baker Women's Center.
April 2009	First annual Sharing the Mantle Conference: what we have learned about multigenerational leadership; modeling broader impact—networking; in the spring. S3! copresents what they have learned about the critical approach to youth-adult partnerships using lessons learned from the Dumpster Project and the CommUNITY Festival.
May 2009	Trip to Chicago: S3! attends "Ella's Daughters" gathering at the University of Illinois, Chicago
June–July 2009	Learn-Teach-Lead workshops
July 2009	Training at Highlander
October 2009	Second annual CommUNITY Festival
	Harm Free Zones Project is launched
November 2009–October 2010	Harm Free Zones community meetings, celebrations, and reflections
	Third annual CommUNITY Festival
Fall 2010	S3! youth attend Moral Monday protests.
April 2011	Second biennial Sharing the Mantle conference
July 2011	New York networking trip—in Ms. Baker's footsteps
August 2011–November 2012	Raise the Age Campaign
December 2012	Family Resource Center is shut down at Regal Gardens
	EBWC moves to center space at Bonner Court.
January 2013–May 2013	Comics Speak! project: partnership with NC Dream Team and local artists
	Third biennial Sharing the Mantle conference
August 2013	March on Washington, DC
August 2013–November 2013	Youth Bridging Cultures project

APPENDIX 2 Curriculum Overview

The Ella Baker Women's Center for Leadership and Community Activism

Striving Sisters Speak! (S3!)
A Model for Teen Girls' Leadership Development for Community-Driven
Social Justice Activism

This curriculum was originally created based on the work of the 2007–2008 S3! cohort and the Ella Baker Women's Center volunteers, students, and staff who partnered with them. The curriculum is grounded in commitments to Ella Baker's legacy of community-driven social justice organizing. It has an organic structure that subsequent S3! cohorts and center staff/volunteers have adapted to meet the needs and desires of the communities with whom we partner.

CRITICAL PEDAGOGICAL FOUNDATIONS FOR TEEN
GIRLS' SOCIAL JUSTICE LEADERSHIP CONTENT

Personal Leadership: learning from the past, present, and future to develop voice, purpose, and community accountability in social justice activism

Organizational Leadership: learning the structures of civic engagement to develop capacities for productive participation and activism

Community Leadership: learning Ella Baker's group-centered approach to community leadership

- Community-driven process to identify, analyze, and research community needs
- Community-driven process to develop, conduct, and evaluate youth-led social justice projects

CORE MODES

Leadership Training: a series of capacity-building training sessions based on critical pedagogy and antiracist activism and rooted in culture and history. Training is structured into modules on personal, organizational, and community leadership capacities, with a focus on developing effective youth-adult partnerships (YAPs) and building multigenerational coalitions for social justice activism within communities and beyond.

Critical Engagement: a series of activities and processes utilizing popular education methods to engage critically with issues of importance, following a *learn-teach-lead model* based on researching the root causes of social justice issues:[1]

Learn: See, analyze, act: excavating concealed stories of social injustice; researching and analyzing their root causes; and building capacity to use a range of actions for activism and change (Boal, 2005).

Teach: Using popular education to teach others about what was learned through the see-analyze-act process.

Lead: Coalitions leading social justice action.

SOCIAL JUSTICE LEADERSHIP TRAINING AND ACTION CYCLE

Phase 1: Social justice leadership training (fourteen weeks/one-day or hybrid three-weekend/weekly training)

Fourteen-week training model (aligns with one semester in the academic school year as after-school program or as a summer program condensed or expanded to fit the needs of the group)

- S3! cohort participants and adult allies participate in fourteen weeks of training (one hour each session, or seven weeks with two-hour sessions) combining leadership capacity building with critical engagement mode, preparing youth for community-based collective action campaigns.
- At the end of the training period, participants convene for a one-day (six-hour) readiness retreat in which they practice facilitation of popular education techniques used throughout their training and develop an action and evaluation plan for activating a multigenerational coalition for a major collective leadership initiative.

Hybrid weekend/weekly training model (aligns with summer program or Friday/Saturday academies throughout the school year)

- S3! cohort participants and adult allies attend **three weekend retreats** focusing on leadership capacity training, with **one weekly meeting in between** based on the critical engagement mode. The **first** of the three retreats focuses on personal development, teamwork, and organizational leadership capacity building. The **second** retreat is intensive community organizing nuts-and-bolts training. The **third** retreat is an action planning retreat, planned and facilitated by youth participants.

- In the **between-retreat meetings**, participants develop political analyses and engagement strategies using *testimonio*, group-centered leadership, participatory research, and radical rehearsal.

Phase 2: Community action, reflection, and evaluation (two to four months)

S3! members and adult allies mobilize a multigenerational coalition for their community-based collective action campaign.

- Collective action can take many forms depending on the insights and interests of the group, including community forums, town hall meetings, social justice theater performance, community film screening, and a resistance campaign.
- Youth and adults reflect on and evaluate the campaign for social impact.

Phase 3: Sustainability

- Start new training cycle while extending the current project, starting a new campaign, or joining other campaigns.
- Trained S3! members serve as **senior youth leaders**, with paid stipends for service in one or more of the following roles:
  ○ recruiting new members for the upcoming training season to build S3! cohort;
  ○ joining the program leadership team (PLT) to help design and facilitate curriculum for the new training cohort, adapting as necessary to reorient the youth-adult partnership and integrate learning and experiences from the ongoing social justice campaigns into the curriculum; and
  ○ forming or joining the community action team (CAT) devoted to furthering community-organizing efforts through leadership and support. The CAT is responsible for offering support to new S3! training cohort participants during their community action campaign, in addition to their own ongoing action campaign(s).

Curriculum Structure for Fourteen-Week + One-Day Training

Note: All training will sustain a focus on creativity, mindfulness, and intersectional sisterhood using the following engagement modalities:

1. Developing and enacting a vision of group-centered intersectional leadership: use art, media, and performance to create a gracious space for learning together; establish shared values, collective vision, processes for participative/group-centered decision-making, accountability, and critical coaching for success.
2. *Testimonio* circles/dialogue circles.
3. Cooperative inquiry/see-analyze-act: When and where does a particular social justice issue come up in our daily lives? What are we taught about these issues by society? By the community? By popular culture? By politicians? By schools?

4. Deepening our connections and analyses: use trips, trainings, film screenings, workshops, and conversation circles with guests and community members to strengthen our bonds and deepen our analysis of capitalism, racism, sexism, class oppression, violence, and resistance.

Personal Leadership (Weeks 1–6)

Module objective: The girls, with guidance from mentors and Ella Baker's legacy of community-led activism, will have the capacity to listen critically and self-reflexively, affirm their activist voices, determine their purposes as social justice activists, and make commitments to making a difference after sharing and learning about the ways power intersects with their personal and cultural histories.

Organizational Leadership (Weeks 7–10)

Module objective: The girls and their adult allies will have the capacity to enact their commitments to effective youth-adult partnerships, based on Ella Baker's group-centered leadership approach, while learning to plan, organize, and lead meetings to effect social justice change.

Community Leadership (Weeks 11–14)

Module objective: The girls and their adult allies will develop communication capacities for enacting the learn-teach-lead approach.

- Learn to **listen for concealed stories of social injustice** through the see-analyze-act process, research and analyze its root causes, and build capacity to use a range of actions for activism and change.
- Learn to **teach others** about what was learned through the see-analyze-act process using popular education tools.
- Learn to **lead coalitions** for social justice action.

Notes

1. Payne (1989), following King (1987), documented that people who worked with Ella Baker always referred to her as "Miss Baker" as a sign of respect. Throughout this book, I use the label "Ms." to remove the implication of patriarchal power that defines women in terms of their legal relationship with men (e.g., "Miss" vs. "Mrs."). In most cases, I simply use her full name or last name.

2. *The Fight for a Right*, an American Public Television documentary produced fifty years after the passage of the 1965 Voting Rights Act, did not mention Ella Baker. There was significant coverage of the Student Nonviolent Coordinating Committee, but there was no reference to Baker's influence on the young people's leadership or her vital role in the founding of the organization and having served as its sole paid staff member during the Mississippi Freedom Summer of 1964.

3. Notably, several prominent celebrities and politicians publicly defended Leslie Jones on Twitter, defined as online platform in Preface (p. xiii). and denounced the actions of internet trolls attacking her. There were structural interventions as well. The Department of Homeland Security investigated the hacking of Jones's website and Twitter banned several of the trolls' accounts (Rogers, 2016). Recently, a graduate student from the School of Education who was enrolled in my seminar on participatory research methods asked how one should respond to queries such as "Why write about Black girls?" I pointed to the

recent spate of news stories about violence against Black girls: at a pool party in Texas one young woman was wrestled to the ground by White police officers, and in another example, a girl was thrown down in her classroom by a school resource officer. Writing about Black girls is a way of writing against narratives that legitimize that violence and otherwise steal their childhoods.

INTRODUCTION

1. "Jamilla" is a pseudonym.
2. The Ella Baker Educational Project of North Carolina was founded by Baker's relatives, who are working to preserve her legacy in eastern North Carolina, including her childhood home (https://ellabakereducationalprojectofnc .org/).
3. Shaw University was founded in 1865 by the American Baptist Home Mission Society, an organization then based in New York City. Like many historically Black colleges, universities, and normal schools founded in the South during the Reconstruction era, Shaw was financed by the Freedman's Bureau, missionary societies, and individual White philanthropists, as well as local Black churches (see Anderson, 1988).
4. See Ransby (2003, p. 55, esp. n. 44).
5. Baker's mother, Anna Ross Baker, had insisted on thirteen-year-old Ella spending an additional year at a local school working with a tutor to prepare her for entry into Shaw Academy.
6. See Ransby (2003, esp. Chapter 8, "Mentoring a New Generation of Activists: The Birth of the Student Nonviolent Coordinating Committee, 1960–1961").
7. I borrow the phrase "new Jim Crow" era from Michelle Alexander's (2010) *The New Jim Crow*. She made a compelling case that the systems of legal segregation and openly racist control tactics, which persisted from Reconstruction through the 1950s in the United States, exist now as the new caste arrangement created by systems of mass incarceration—targeting primarily youth of color—and sustained by subtle systemic racism. It was she who popularized the phrase "the New Jim Crow." Others have described these structured systems of oppression and the social-psychological forces that keep them in place. For example, Young (2001) wrote about the "birdcage" metaphor to explain structural racism; Cohen (2001) described the personal and political ways uncomfortable realities are avoided and evaded; and Beckett and Herbert (2010) wrote that many US cities employ social control tools—gang injunctions, no-contact laws, or simply banning people from being within a specified target area—that fuse civil and criminal law to accomplish spatial exclusion. I use these and other sources in this book to explain and theorize a particular moment that is catalyzing a response—

perhaps fragmented and not clearly identifiable as a movement—but nevertheless a moment pregnant with possibilities for inspired youth leadership.

8. The names of the housing complexes are pseudonyms.

9. "College Town" is a pseudonym for the city where this case study took place, in the research triangle area of North Carolina. The area is home to three college towns in close proximity: Raleigh, Durham, and Chapel Hill. These cities are in many ways very similar to college towns across the United States where predominantly White universities are situated near historically Black communities, creating racialized dynamics that play out as inequities in education, housing, and employment.

10. Gwen Ifill was an African American female journalist who was the moderator and managing editor of *Washington Week*, which appears on Public Broadcasting Service (PBS) stations in the United States, as well as the coanchor and managing editor of *PBS NewsHour*. She was also the best-selling author of *The Breakthrough: Politics and Race in the Age of Obama* (Doubleday, 2009).

11. The UNC–Chapel Hill provost has convened two task forces to establish tenure and promotion guidelines for engaged scholarship. The first, in 2010, resulted in a set of guidelines that came into effect in 2013. Later, the university's academic promotion and tenure committee requested more specificity in the guidelines. In 2016, a second task force was convened that established a new set of guidelines that differentiated community-engaged scholarship from public scholarship.

12. The center was established with support from the Kauffman Foundation's Faculty Fellowship for Social Entrepreneurship at the University of North Carolina at Chapel Hill (UNC–Chapel Hill) and the UNC School of Government.

13. "Ms. Vergie" is a pseudonym.

14. Holsaert et al. (2010).

15. For a comprehensive account, see Kay Mills's excellent biography of Fannie Lou Hamer, *This Little Light of Mine: The Life of Fannie Lou Hamer* (University Press of Kentucky, 2007).

CHAPTER 1. TRANSLATING ELLA BAKER'S LEGACY OF SOCIAL JUSTICE LEADERSHIP INTO EVERYDAY PRAXIS

1. This analysis builds on Barbara Ransby's observation that, in comparing Baker to Gramsci, a European male philosopher, her purpose was *not* to perpetuate a practice of subsuming Black thinkers and theorists under White ones in order to legitimate them. Rather, her intention was to illustrate the parallels between Gramsci's and Baker's thinking. Baker's approach emerged from her political experimentation; it was not based on the influence of Gramsci's thinking (see Ransby, 2003, p. 419).

2. A testament to the veracity of Gramsci's philosophy of praxis is the wide sphere of influence—across disciplines, cultures, and geographies—in which that philosophy has been taken up. Still, it would be intriguing to know how he might have applied his own methods in concrete contexts.

3. This analysis is based on a close archival reading of the literature on Ella Baker's life and legacy, drawing on the several biographies and book chapters written about her, especially Ransby's (2003) comprehensive volume. I also studied the Ella Baker Papers at the Schomburg Center for Research in Black Culture, the digital archives at the University of Wisconsin, and films and recordings documenting interviews with Ms. Baker. The analysis is also based on my own field-testing of her ideas in my years of participatory research with African American girls enacting social justice leadership. The Gramscian analysis relies heavily on my study of Gramsci's prison notebooks (Gramsci, 1992–2007), guided by scholarly interpretations from Buttigieg (1995), Crehan (2002, 2016), Golding (1992), and Thomas (2009). I am grateful to Dottie Holland for the hours we spent during summer 2014, thinking and writing together about Gramsci's ideas.

4. Importantly, Gramsci distinguishes "organic intellectuals" from "traditional intellectuals," who occupy elite positions within power structures and (wittingly or not) have vested interests in the reproduction of the status quo (see Mumby, 1997, for one interpretation of that distinction from his perspective as a self-described organic intellectual).

5. Gramsci's critique of Machiavellianism is, I think, the most elegant argument for teaching the "rules" of the workings of power to the masses. If Machiavelli's prince was being instructed on the workings of power—helped to be "in the know" about how state power works—then organic intellectuals should also be in the know about how to dismantle and transform state power into a new hegemony.

6. Prefigurative politics "refers to a political orientation based on the premise that the ends a social movement achieves are fundamentally shaped by the means it employs, and that movements should therefore do their best to choose means that embody or 'prefigure' the kind of society they want to bring about" (Leach, 2013, p. 1004).

7. As I edit this chapter for publication, there is breaking news of the arrest of billionaire hedge fund manager Jeffrey Epstein for alleged international sex trafficking of girls as young as fourteen (Mazzei & Rashbaum, 2019).

8. The view of violence as a complex phenomenon is consistent with that of contemporary peace and justice movements, such as restorative justice. Critical Resistance, an organization founded by Angela Davis in the 1970s as a prison abolitionist movement, provides these definitions of intrapersonal, interpersonal, systemic, and institutional violence:

By "inter-personal harm" we mean a harm done to a person by another (for example, someone beating someone else). By "intra-communal harm" we mean harms done to community members that a community condones by doing nothing about it (for example, the communal silence that surrounds incest), or harms that are perpetrated by the community on its members often with the backup of the state (for example, ostracizing members of gangs). Intra-social harms refers to harms perpetrated by the larger society either directly or through condoning harms perpetrated by individuals, groups, communities, or the state (for example: creating health risks through pollution; massive sterilization of people of color; or racism, which is a harm that is done person to person, by the state, by groups, and in the organization of the economy). Often interpersonal harm is possible because it occurs within a communal and social environment that backs up, or calls forth, or even rewards it. It is important that as we intervene in particular cases of harm, we do not focus solely on the inter-personal, but also on the intra-communal and intra-social factors. (Critical Resistance, 2014, p. 1, n. 1)

CHAPTER 2. "PEOPLE UNDER THE HEELS OF OPPRESSION SHOULD BE THE ONES LEADING": ENTERING INTO COMMUNITY PARTNERSHIPS

1. Ella Baker, interview by John Britton, June 19, 1968, Civil Rights Oral History Project, Moorland-Springarn Research Center, Howard University, Washington, DC, p. 82. Quoted in Ransby (2003, pp. 305–306).

2. As a student organizer at Ohio Wesleyan University, Mary King had organized a student committee on race relations in solidarity with Black students and their allies leading the sit-in movements. After King's graduation in 1962, Ella Baker offered her an internship at the Atlanta-based Young Women's Christian Association (YWCA). In this role, "King traveled to White institutions across the South initiating discussions about race relations under the rubric of conversations on academic freedom. She organized interracial workshops that deconstructed systems of race and racism" (Legacy Project & Duke University, n.d.).

3. See Holsaert et al. (2010) for a comprehensive account of women's experiences as SNCC organizers.

4. This understanding follows closely with Gramsci's philosophy of praxis grounded in the contingent: social strategy and specifics of social truth. Social strategy and social truth both express and constitute reality. This is the political moment, when the possibility of change happens. Baker was always seeking those moments. (This should not be confused with simply joining a protest in direct action, or even finding a way to subvert power temporarily: weak power, à la Michel de Certeau.)

5. Tonn (2003) provided excellent context for Mary Parker Follett's prescient books *The New State* (1918) and *Creative Experience* (1924). She wrote that Follett's opus about cooperation, power, and engaging human capacity in business, published during the rise of the Industrial Revolution, was

informed by insights gained from twenty years of civic and professional work in Boston's immigrant neighborhoods. Through projects developed for the Boston Equal Suffrage Association for Good Government and the Women's Municipal League of Boston, Follett honed her formidable entrepreneurial, political, managerial, and fundraising skills and became an inspiring mentor to a new generation of Boston civic leaders. Dissatisfied with the efforts of the neighborhood settlements and the public schools to foster community, Follett slowly evolved a new approach to preparing Boston's newest citizens for their civic responsibilities: she created organizations in which they could govern their own activities and, thereby, prepare for participation in democratic government. (Tonn, 2003, p. 5)

Follett's insight laid the foundation for the dynamic principles of coactive process in organizing discussed here.

6. Both names are pseudonyms.

7. I first heard the phrase, "calling in" versus "calling out" in my decolonizing methodologies course. A student, Adébukola Oni, used it in our class to signify the community we had created in the classroom and to show that we are all called in to be accountable to each other.

8. The AME Women's Missionary Society is not part of the tradition of White colonial mission trips to indigenous countries. Rather, it is an important part of nineteenth-century Black women's history of philanthropy and mutual aid societies. My participation at my church carried with it a belief in the traditions of liberation theology that focused on mission work as grounded in structural analyses of power and advancing freedom from oppression.

9. Ms. Naomi was most likely referring to researchers from the Frank Porter Graham Child Development Institute, the highly recognized program at the University of North Carolina at Chapel Hill, which conducts research on early childhood education. The Family Resource Center programs had been the site for one or more of the institute's studies.

10. Housing policies in the United States have become discursive sites for control of Black women through impossible-to-follow rules as conditions for residency, which in turn make their families even more vulnerable to the impacts of economic and housing insecurity. This is discussed further in chapter 3, following the work of Crenshaw (2013) and Williams (2004).

11. The young women's activist group and their social justice projects are discussed more fully in chapter 3.

CHAPTER 3. "THINK IN RADICAL TERMS":
CREATING PARTICIPATIVE SPACES FOR SOCIAL
JUSTICE ORGANIZING

1. The cultural studies theorist Larry Grossberg explained how context serves as a productive framing tool: "Contexts animate agents and actions; things are

made possible, thinkable, desirable, or necessary by the conjunction of many contexts. As such, this requires a type of analysis that is particular, contextually sensitive, and concrete: not necessarily 'local' (since the scale of contexts and actions varies), but avoiding decontextualizing, or empty, abstraction. . . . Within any given space, such contexts are always plural. Moreover, within any context, as a result of its complex relations to other contexts, power is always multidimensional, contradictory, and never sewn up" (quoted in Clarke, 2011, p. 311).

2. This section was excerpted from an essay that Elisa, Joaquín, and I published in 2011 (see Parker et al., 2011).

3. Ms. Vergie (personal communication, 2008).

4. "AmeriCorps is a network of national service programs, made up of three primary programs that each take a different approach to improving lives and fostering civic engagement. Members commit their time to address critical community needs like increasing academic achievement, mentoring youth, fighting poverty, sustaining national parks, preparing for disasters, and more" (AmeriCorps, n.d.).

5. Pseudonyms are used for the girls and others from the neighborhoods.

6. "Calling in" seems like an appropriate way to describe the community S3! was building.

7. Both Joaquín and Elisa were on deadlines to produce a research paper. Elisa's paper would be based in part on the *testimonio* sessions with the girls, which were separate from our meetings; Joaquín's paper was based on the organizing structure, so making a decision to hold to a flexible structure informed his theorizing about social justice organizing.

8. This way of framing urban Black girls and women's social location is borrowed from Hicks's (2010) excellent account of working-class Black women in early twentieth-century New York City.

CHAPTER 4. "STRONG PEOPLE DON'T NEED STRONG LEADERS": ENGAGING SOCIAL JUSTICE STORYTELLING FOR CATALYTIC LEADERSHIP

1. This section draws heavily from Bell (2010, pp. 22–25).

2. Sonny Kelly's one-man performance *The Talk* powerfully illustrates how concealed stories about police harassment are deployed for social justice across multiple scales (individual, family, and societal) (see Kelly, 2018).

3. On August 11, 1961, there was a heated discussion about whether the still-emerging SNCC should focus on direct action desegregation campaigns or on voter registration drives in the Deep South. Ella Baker provided a way forward as she counseled the group (see Ransby, 2003).

4. These statistics are reported in Fieldhouse (2013). My field notes from 2009 referenced the concentrated wealth in the top 1 percent of households in

the United States but did not mention the source provided in the materials from Highlander.

5. As of this writing, the Harm Free Zones (HFZ) movement continues under the leadership of SpiritHouse, which is catalyzing grassroots action at the local, state, and national levels. Founded in 1999, SpiritHouse is a Black women–led collective based in Durham, North Carolina, that uses art, culture, and media to support the empowerment and transformation of communities most impacted by racism, poverty, gender inequity, criminalization, and incarceration.

6. The previously concealed stories of police harassment and violence in Black and Brown communities have steadily come to light with the rise of social media. In 2014, after the killing of Michael Brown and the reports on social media and news outlets documenting the violence against Black and Brown people being arrested, too often resulting in their death, White people on social media started reporting their experiences with the police, which were in stark contrast to that violence. The 2015 arrest of Dylan Roof, the White supremacist who murdered nine people at Emanuel African Methodist Episcopal Church, is one example of that double standard; it is powerfully depicted in the 2019 documentary *Emanuel* (Shepherd et al., 2019).

7. In 2014, NC Action for Children merged with the Covenant with NC's Children to create NC Child (https://www.ncchild.org/).

8. "Lydia" is a pseudonym.

CHAPTER 5. REWRITING ELLA BAKER'S DAYBOOK: INTEGRATING SELF-CARE AND ACTIVIST WORK

1. In addition to Ella Baker's daybook, archived at the Schomburg Library in Harlem, this section relies heavily on Ransby's (2003) archival reading of Baker's time as NAACP field secretary (see esp. pp. 104–31).

2. Wesley Hogan, interview with Muriel Tillinghast, April 13, 2000, SNCC Fortieth Anniversary (DVD2).

3. This chapter is written from the perspective of my lived experience as a cis-gendered Black woman with a PhD at an elite university attempting to do community-accountable scholarship. The meanings of self-care for S3! and others in this book's accounting of the work we did together are theirs to tell.

CONCLUSION

1. Notably, the Black Lives Matter movement and the larger coalition that is the Movement for Black Lives have championed the grassroots, group-centered approach to leadership akin to what Ella Baker taught (see Ransby, 2017). Two

other youth-led movements are getting media attention as of this writing. Five students and their allies from the Marjory Stoneman Douglas High School in Parkland, Florida, started the Never Again movement after seventeen people were killed and another seventeen injured in a mass shooting at their school (see Alter, 2018). The youth-led movement has rallied anti-NRA, anti-gun-violence activists in the United States. Globally, seventeen-year-old Greta Thunberg, a Swedish climate activist, has become a spokesperson for her generation. It would be worth investigating whether and how a group-centered catalyzing leadership approach is fueling these grassroots movements in addition to the very visible leaders.

2. The term *nonprofit* is used in the US context to denote a distinction in the tax code.

3. As noted in Barinaga and Parker (2013), university-community scholarship gained momentum following the plea from Ernest L. Boyer, the former president of the Carnegie Foundation, about "connecting the rich resources of the university to our most pressing social, civic, and ethical problems, to our children, to our schools, to our teachers, and to our cities" (1996, pp. 19–20). Particularly in North America, Boyer's plea sparked a movement of scholarly efforts to engage with the most disenfranchised communities beyond university campuses (see, e.g., Imagining America, a collaboration of about one hundred universities and colleges that promotes engaged scholarship through research, teaching, and learning; http://imaginingamerica.org).

APPENDIX 2

1. Rachel Valentine, Public Allies fellow, 2009–2010, and Dr. Patricia S. Parker, founder/director, Ella Baker Women's Center, created the "learn-teach-lead" concept in 2009.

References

Action for Children North Carolina. (2013). *From push out to lock out: North Carolina's accelerated school-to-prison pipeline*. Raleigh, NC: Action for Children NC.

Ahmed, S. (2012). *On being included: Racism and diversity in institutional life*. Durham, NC: Duke University Press.

Alexander, M. (2010). *The New Jim Crow: Mass incarceration in the age of colorblindness*. New York: The New Press.

Alter, C. (2018, March 22). The school shooting generation has had enough. *Time*. https://time.com/longform/never-again-movement/

AmeriCorps. (n.d.). What is AmeriCorps? https://www.nationalservice.gov/programs/americorps/what-americorps

Anderson, J. D. (1988). *The education of blacks in the South, 1860–1935*. Chapel Hill: University of North Carolina Press.

Anheier, H. K. (2014). *Nonprofit organizations: Theory, management, policy* (2nd ed.). New York: Routledge.

Argyris, C., & Schön, D. A. (1996). *Organizational learning II: Theory, method and practice*. Reading, MA: Addison-Wesley.

Bailey, M., & Trudy. (2018). On misogynoir: Citation, erasure, and plagiarism. *Feminist Media Studies*, *18*(4), 762–768. https://doi.org/10.1080/14680777.2018.1447395

Baker, E. (1960). Bigger than a hamburger. *Southern Patriot*, *18*(5), 4.

Baker, E. (1999). Interview by Joanne Grant (1969). In J. Grant, *Ella Baker: Freedom bound* (p. 230). New York: Wiley.

Baker, E. (1972). Developing community leadership. In G. Lerner (Ed.), *Black women in white America: A documentary history* (pp. 345–352). New York: Pantheon.

Baker, E. (1977, April 19). Interview by Casey Hayden and Sue Thrasher. New York: Southern Oral History Program, University of North Carolina, Chapel Hill.

Baker, E. (1980). Organizing for civil rights: Interview with Ellen Cantarow and Susan Gushee O'Malley. In E. Cantarow (Ed.), *Moving the mountain* (pp. 52–93). Old Westbury, NY: The Feminist Press.

Baker, E. (2017). Keynote speech before the state convention of the Mississippi Democratic Freedom Party, August 6, 1964. In J. Dittmer, J. Kolnick, & L. McLemore (Eds.), *Freedom Summer: A brief history with documents* (p. 31). Boston: Bedford/St. Martin's.

Baker, E., & Cooke, M. (1935, November). The Bronx slave market. *Crisis, 42*, 330–331, 340.

Baker, L. T. (2005). Freeing ourselves from neocolonial domination in research: A Kaupapa Māori approach to creating knowledge. In N. K. Denzin & Y. S. Lincoln (Eds.), *The Sage handbook of qualitative research* (3rd ed., pp. 109–138). Thousand Oaks, CA: Sage Publications.

Banet-Weiser, S., & Miltner, K. M. (2016). #MasculinitySoFragile: Culture, structure, and networked misogyny. *Feminist Media Studies, 16*(1), 171–174. https://doi.org/10.1080/14680777.2016.1120490

Barge, J. K. (2006). Practical theory as mapping, engaged reflection, and transformative practice. *Communication Theory, 11*(1), 5–13.

Barinaga, E., & Parker, P. S. (2013). Community-engaged scholarship: Creating participative spaces for transformative politics. *Tamara: Journal for Critical Organization Inquiry, 11*(4), 5–11.

Beckett, K., & Herbert, S. K. (2010). *Banished: The transformation of urban social control.* New York: Oxford University Press.

Bell, D. A. (1995). Who's afraid of critical race theory? *University of Illinois Law Review, 1995*(4), 893–910.

Bell, E. L., & Nkomo, S. M. (2001). *Our separate ways: Black and white women and the struggle for professional identity.* Cambridge, MA: Harvard Business Press.

Bell, L. A. (2010). *Storytelling for social justice: Connecting narrative and the arts in antiracist teaching.* New York: Routledge.

Bell, L. A., Roberts, R. A., Irani, K., & Murphy, B. (2008). *The storytelling project curriculum: Learning about race and racism through storytelling and the arts.* New York: Barnard College. http://www.racialequitytools.org/resourcefiles/stp_curriculum.pdf

Bhattacharyya, J. (2004). Theorizing community development. *Journal of the Community Development Society, 34*(2), 5–34. https://doi.org/10.1080/15575330409490110

Block, P. (2008). *Community: The structure of belonging.* San Francisco: Berrett-Koehler.

Boal, A. (2005). *Games for actors and non-actors.* New York: Routledge.

Bowerman, M. (2017, December 13). Twitter thanks #BlackWomen for voting for democrat Doug Jones in Alabama Senate election. *USA Today.* https://www.usatoday.com/story/news/politics/onpolitics/2017/12/13/twitter-thanksblackwomen-voting-democrat-doug-jones-alabama-senate-election/947403001/

Boyer, E. (1996). The scholarship of engagement. *Journal of Public Service and Outreach, 1*(1), 11–20.

Branch, T. (2007). *Parting the waters: America in the King years, 1954–63.* New York: Simon and Schuster. (Original work published 1988)

Brown, A. M. (2017). *Emergent strategy: Shaping change, changing worlds.* Chico, CA: AK Press.

Brown, R. N. (2013). *Hear our truths: The creative potential of Black girlhood.* Urbana: University of Illinois Press.

Brown, W. (2015). *Undoing the demos: Neoliberalism's stealth revolution.* Cambridge, MA: MIT Press.

Butler, O. E. (2012). *Parable of the Sower* (Vol. 1). New York: Open Road Media.

Buttigieg, J. A. (1995). Gramsci on civil society. *boundary 2, 22*(3), 1–32.

Buttigieg, J. A. (2011). Chronology. In J. A. Buttigieg (Ed.), *Antonio Gramsci: Prison notebooks* (Vol. 1, pp. 64–94). New York: Columbia University Press. (Original work published 1972)

Camacho, M. M. (2004). Power and privilege: Community service learning in Tijuana. *Michigan Journal of Community Service Learning, 10*(3), 31–42.

Cantarow, E. (1980). *Moving the mountain: Women working for social change.* Old Westbury, NY: Feminist Press.

Chakrabarty, D. (2002). *Habitations of modernity: Essays in the wake of subaltern studies.* Chicago: University of Chicago Press.

Chun, J. J., Lipsitz, G., & Shin, Y. (2013). Intersectionality as a social movement strategy: Asian immigrant women advocates. *Signs, 38*(4), 917–940.

Clarke, J. (2011). Tense futures: The work of cultural studies. *Communication and Critical/Cultural Studies, 8*(3), 309–313.

Clarke, J. (2015). Stuart Hall and the theory and practice of articulation. *Discourse: Studies in the Cultural Politics of Education, 36*(2), 275–286.

Coates, T.-N. (2014, June). The case for reparations. *The Atlantic.* https://www.theatlantic.com/magazine/archive/2014/06/the-case-for-reparations/361631/

Cohen, J. (2004, October 27). A silent epidemic: Why is there such a high percentage of HIV and AIDS among black women? *Slate*. https://slate.com/technology/2004/10/black-women-and-aids.html

Cohen, S. (2001). *States of denial*. Malden, MA: Polity.

Cole, T. (2012, March 21). The white-savior industrial complex. *The Atlantic*. https://www.theatlantic.com/international/archive/2012/03/the-white-savior-industrial-complex/254843/

Collins, P. H. (1989). The social construction of invisibility: Black women's poverty in social problems discourse. *Perspectives on Social Problems, 1*, 77–93.

Collins, P. H. (1990). Black feminist thought in the matrix of domination. *Black feminist thought: Knowledge, consciousness, and the politics of empowerment, 138*, 221–238.

Collins, P. H. (1998). *Fighting words: Black women and the search for justice*. Minneapolis: University of Minnesota Press.

Collins, P. H., & Bilge, S. (2016). *Intersectionality*. Medford, MA: Polity Press.

Crehan, K. (2002). *Gramsci, culture and anthropology*. Berkeley: University of California Press.

Crehan, K. (2016). *Gramsci's common sense: Inequality and its narratives*. Durham, NC: Duke University Press.

Crenshaw, K. W. (2013). From private violence to mass incarceration: Thinking intersectionally about women, race, and social control. *Journal of Scholarly Perspectives, 9*(1), 23–50.

Critical Resistance. (2014, May). *Harm Free Zone project: General framework*. Oakland, CA: Author. http://criticalresistance.org/wp-content/uploads/2014/05/HFZ-NY.pdf

Critical Resistance. (2018, December). 20 years of CR: Celebrating our success, funding our future. http://criticalresistance.org/celebrating-our-success-funding-our-future/

Cruz, J. M. (2017). Invisibility and visibility in alternative organizing: A communicative and cultural model. *Management Communication Quarterly, 31*(4), 614–639.

Daniels, J. (2009). *Cyber racism: White supremacy online and the new attack on civil rights*. Lanham, MD: Rowman & Littlefield.

Daniels, L., Magness, G., & Siegel-Magness, S. (Producers), & Daniels, L. (Director). (2009). *Precious: Based on the novel "Push" by Sapphire* [Film]. Lionsgate.

Davies, C. B., Gadsby, M., Peterson, C. F., & Williams, H. (2003). *Decolonizing the academy: African diaspora studies*. Trenton, NJ: Africa World Press.

Davis, A. Y. (1990). Sick and tired of being sick and tired: The politics of black women's health. In A. Y. Davis (Ed.), *Women, culture, politics* (p. 54). New York: Vintage. (Original work published 1984)

Davis, A., & Edwards, S. (2019). *Freedom is rest* [Videotaped live performance]. Centro Cultural Larinda Santos Lobo, Santa Teresa, Rio de Janeiro, Brazil.

Dawson, M. C. (1995). *Behind the mule: Race and class in African-American politics*. Princeton, NJ: Princeton University Press.

Deetz, S. A. (1992). *Democracy in an age of corporate colonization: Developments in communication and the politics of everyday life*. Albany: State University of New York Press.

DeLaure, M. B. (2008). Planting seeds of change: Ella Baker's radical rhetoric. *Women's Studies in Communication, 31*(1), 1–28.

Dempsey, S. E. (2007). Negotiating accountability within international contexts: The role of bounded voice. *Communication Monographs, 74*(3), 311–332.

Dempsey, S. E., & Barge, J. K. (2014). Engaged scholarship and democracy. In L. L. Putnam & D. K. Mumby (Eds.), *The Sage handbook of organizational communication* (3rd ed., pp. 665–688). Thousand Oaks, CA: Sage Publications.

Dutta, M. J. (2011). *Communicating social change: Structure, culture, and agency*. New York: Routledge.

Dutta, M. J. (2015). Decolonizing communication for social change: A culture-centered approach. *Communication Theory, 25*(2), 123–143.

Edwards-Levy, A. (2017, March 30). Progressive activism has surged since Donald Trump took office. HuffPost. https://www.huffpost.com/entry/progressive-activism-surge-donald-trump-took-office_n_58dd8950e4b0e6ac7093b3c1

Ekers, M., Hart, G., Kipfer, S., & Loftus, A. (Eds.). (2012). *Gramsci: Space, nature, politics*. Malden, MA: Wiley-Blackwell.

Election 2008: South Carolina primary results. (2016, December 6). *The New York Times*. https://www.nytimes.com/elections/2008/primaries/results/states/SC.html

Eliasoph, N. (2013). *Making volunteers: Civic life after welfare's end* (Vol. 50). Princeton, NJ: Princeton University Press.

Fieldhouse, A. (2013, June 14). *Rising income inequality and the role of shifting market-income distribution, tax burdens, and tax rates* (Issue Brief No. 365). Economic Policy Institute. https://www.epi.org/publication/rising-income-inequality-role-shifting-market/

Fine, M. (1994). Dis-stance and other stances: Negotiations of power inside feminist research. In A. Gitlin (Ed.), *Power and method: Political activism and educational research* (pp. 13–35). New York: Routledge.

Fine, M., & Weis, L. (1998). *The unknown city: The lives of poor and working-class young adults*. Boston: Beacon Press.

Follett, M. P. (1918). *The new state: Group organization the solution of popular government*. New York: Longmans, Green.

Follett, M. P. (1924). *Creative experience*. New York: Longmans, Green.

Fosl, C. (2008). Anne Braden, Fannie Lou Hamer, and Rigoberta Menchu: Using personal narrative to build activist movements. In R. Solinger, M. Fox, & I. Irani (Eds.), *Telling stories to change the world: Global voices on the power of narrative to build community and make social justice claims* (pp. 217–226). New York: Routledge.

Foucault, M. (1977). *Discipline and punish: The birth of the prison* (A. Sheridan, Trans.). New York: Vintage.

Freire, P. (1970). *Pedagogy of the oppressed*. New York: Herder and Herder.

Furco, A. (1996). Service-learning: A balanced approach to experiential education. In B. Taylor & Corporation for National Service (Eds.), *Expanding boundaries: Serving and learning* (pp. 2–6). Washington, DC: Corporation for National Service.

Gallent, N. (2014). Connecting to the citizenry? Support groups in community planning in England. In N. Gallent & D. Ciaffi (Eds.), *Community action and planning: Contexts, drivers and outcomes* (pp. 301–322). Bristol: Policy Press.

Galston, W.A. (2018, January 10). Data point to a new wave of female political activism that could shift the course of US politics. Brookings Institute. https://www.brookings.edu/blog/fixgov/2018/01/10/a-new-wave-of-female-political-activism/

Gardinier, L. (2017). Colleges and universities: Structure and role in civil society. In L. Gardiner (Ed.), *Service learning through community engagement: What community partners and members gain, lose, and learn from campus collaborations* (pp. 9–19). New York: Springer Publications.

Garza, A. (2014, October 7). A herstory of the #BlackLivesMatter movement. *The Feminist Wire*. https://thefeministwire.com/2014/10/blacklivesmatter-2/

Geiger, R.L. (2014). *The history of American higher education: Learning and culture from the founding to World War II*. Princeton, NJ: Princeton University Press.

Giddings, P.J. (1984). *When and where I enter: The impact of black women on race and sex in America*. New York: W. Morrow.

Gilkes, C.T. (1980). Holding back the ocean with a broom: Black women and community work. In L.F. Rodgers-Rose (Ed.), *The black woman* (pp. 217–232). Beverly Hills, CA: Sage.

Ginwright, S.A. (2010). *Black youth rising: Activism and radical healing in urban America*. New York: Teachers College Press.

Giovanni, N. (1994). *Racism 101*. New York: W. Morrow.

Goldenberg, S. (2014, July 14). Eight ways climate change is making the world more dangerous. *The Guardian*. https://www.theguardian.com/environment/blog/2014/jul/14/8-charts-climate-change-world-more-dangerous

Golding, S. (1992). *Gramsci's democratic theory: Contributions to a post-liberal democracy.* Toronto: University of Toronto Press.

Gordon Nembhard, J. (2004). Cooperative ownership in the struggle for African American economic empowerment. *Humanity & Society, 28*(3), 298–321.

Gordon Nembhard, J. (2014). *Collective courage: A history of African American cooperative economic thought and practice.* University Park: Pennsylvania State University Press.

Gramsci, A. (1992–2007). *Prison notebooks* (Vols. 1–3) (J. A. Buttigieg, Ed. and Trans.). New York: Columbia University Press.

Gramsci, A. (1993). *Letters from prison* (Vol. 1) (F. A. Rosengarten, Ed.; R. Rosenthal, Trans.). New York: Columbia University Press.

Grant, J. (1998). *Ella Baker: Freedom bound.* New York: Wiley & Sons.

Greenleaf, R. K. (1977). *Servant leadership: A journey into the nature of legitimate power and greatness.* New York: Paulist Press.

Grossberg, L. (2010). *Cultural studies in the future tense.* Durham, NC: Duke University Press.

Guinier, L., & Torres, G. (2009). *The miner's canary: Enlisting race, resisting power, transforming democracy.* Cambridge, MA: Harvard University Press.

Gumbs, A. P. (2016). *Spill: Scenes of black feminist fugitivity.* Durham, NC: Duke University Press.

Hale, C. R. (2001). What is activist research? *Social Science Research Council, 2*(1–2), 13–15.

Hall, J. D. (1983). The mind that burns in each body: Women, rape, and racial violence. In A. Snitow, C. Stansell, & S. Thompson (Eds.), *Powers of desire: The politics of sexuality* (pp. 328–349). New York: Monthly Review Press.

Hall, S. (1987, June). Gramsci and us. *Marxism Today,* 16–21.

Hardy, C., Phillips, N., & Lawrence, T. B. (2003). Resources, knowledge, and influence: The organizational effects of interorganizational collaboration. *Journal of Management Studies, 40*(2), 321–347.

Hartnett, S. J. (Ed.). (2011). *Challenging the prison-industrial complex: Activism, arts, and educational* alternatives. Urbana: University of Illinois Press.

Heywood, A. (1994). *Political ideas and concepts: An introduction.* London: Macmillan.

Hicks, C. D. (2010). *Talk with you like a woman: African American women, justice, and reform in New York, 1890–1935.* Chapel Hill: University of North Carolina Press.

Hine, D. C., King, W., & Reed, L. (Eds.) (1995). *"We specialize in the wholly impossible": A reader in black women's history.* Brooklyn, NY: Carlson Publishing.

Hohle, R. (2013). *Black citizenship and authenticity in the civil rights movement.* New York: Routledge.

Holsaert, F. S., Noonan, M. P. N., Richardson, J., Robinson, B. G., Young, J. S., & Zellner, D. M. (Eds.). (2010). *Hands on the freedom plow: Personal accounts by women in SNCC*. Urbana: University of Illinois Press.

hooks, b. (1989). *Talking back: Thinking feminist, thinking black*. Boston: South End Press.

Horton, M., & Freire, P. (1990). *We make the road by walking: Conversations on education and social change* (B. Bell, J. Gaventa, & J. Peters, Eds.). Philadelphia: Temple University Press.

House, R. J. (1996). Path-goal theory of leadership: Lessons, legacy, and a reformulated theory. *The Leadership Quarterly, 7*(3), 323–352.

Howard, A. (2016, August 26). Why was Leslie Jones targeted by trolls? *NBC News*. https://www.nbcnews.com/news/us-news/why-was-leslie-jones-targeted-trolls-n638291

Inglehart, R., & Norris, P. (2016, August). *Trump, Brexit, and the rise of populism: Economic have-nots and cultural backlash* (HKS Working Paper No. RWP16-026). Harvard Kennedy School. https://www.hks.harvard.edu/publications/trump-brexit-and-rise-populism-economic-have-nots-and-cultural-backlash

Itkowitz, C. (2019, July 27). Trump attacks Rep. Cummings's district calling it a 'disgusting, rat and rodent infested mess.' *The Washington Post*. https://www.washingtonpost.com/politics/trump-attacks-rep-cummingss-district-calling-it-a-disgusting-rat-and-rodent-infested-mess/2019/07/27/b93c89b2-b073-11e9-bc5c-e73b603e7f38_story.html

James, J. (1994). Ella Baker, 'black women's work' and activist intellectuals. *The Black Scholar, 24*(4), 8–15. https://doi.org/10.1080/00064246.1994.11413167

Jensen, R. J., & Hammerback, J. C. (2000). Working in "quiet places": The community organizing rhetoric of Robert Parris Moses. *Howard Journal of Communication, 11*(1), 1–18. https://doi.org/10.1080/106461700246689

Kellogg Foundation. (2007). The collective leadership framework: A workbook for cultivating and sustaining community change. Battle Creek, MI: W. K. Kellogg Foundation.

Kelly, S. (2018, September 23). *"The Talk" trailer* [Video]. YouTube. https://www.youtube.com/watch?v=3t1uxPkyjSk

King, M. E. (1987). *Freedom song: A personal story of the 1960s civil rights movement*. New York: William Morrow & Co.

King, T. (2014, June). Labor's aphasia: Toward antiblackness as constitutive to settler colonialism. *Decolonization: Indigeneity, Education & Society*. https://decolonization.wordpress.com/2014/06/10/labors-aphasia-toward-antiblackness-as-constitutive-to-settler-colonialism.

Kipfer, S. (2008). How Lefebvre urbanized Gramsci: Hegemony, everyday life, and difference. In K. Goonewardena, S. Kipfer, R. Milgrom, & C. Schmid

(Eds.), *Space, difference, everyday life: Reading Henri Lefebvre* (pp. 207–225). New York: Routledge.

Kwon, S. A. (2013). *Uncivil youth: Race, activism, and affirmative governmentality*. Durham, NC: Duke University Press.

Lather, P. (1986). Research as praxis. *Harvard Educational Review, 56*(3), 257–278.

Lawson, C. E. (2018). Platform vulnerabilities: Harassment and misogynoir in the digital attack on Leslie Jones. *Information, Communication & Society, 21*(6), 818–833.

Leach, D. K. (2013). Prefigurative politics. In D. A. Snow, D. della Porta, B. Klandermans, & D. McAdam (Eds.), *The Wiley-Blackwell encyclopedia of social and political movements* (pp. 1004–1005). Malden, MA: Wiley.

Legacy Project & Duke University. (n.d.). Mary King. *SNCC Digital Gateway.* https://snccdigital.org/people/mary-king/

Lerner, G. (1974). Early community work of black club women. *The Journal of Negro History, 59*(2), 158–167.

Lipsitz, G. (2012). "In an avalanche every snowflake pleads not guilty": The collateral consequences of mass incarceration and impediments to women's fair housing rules. *UCLA Law Review, 59*(6), 1746–1809.

Lipsky, M. (1980). *Street-level bureaucracy: Dilemmas of the individual in public services*. New York: Russell Sage.

Liu, E. (2017, March 8). How Donald Trump is reviving American democracy. *The Atlantic.* https://www.theatlantic.com/politics/archive/2017/03/how-donald-trump-is-reviving-our-democracy/518928/

Lofquist, W. A. (1989). *The technology of prevention workbook: A leadership development program*. Tucson, AZ: AYD Publications.

Lorde, A. (1978). Uses of the erotic: The erotic as power. In *Sister outsider: Essays and speeches* (pp. 53–59). Berkeley, CA: Crossing Press.

Lorde, A. (1995). *The black unicorn: Poems*. New York: Norton.

Lorde, A. (2006). *The cancer journals*. San Francisco, CA: Aunt Lute. (Original work published 1980)

Love, B., & Duncan, K. E. (2017). Put some respect on our name: Why every black & brown girl needs to learn about radical feminist leadership. *Occasional Paper Series, 2017*(38), 7.

Lucaites, J. L., & Condit, C. M. (1990). Reconstructing <equality>: Culturetypal and counter-cultural rhetorics in the martyred black vision. *Communication Monographs, 57*(1), 5–24.

Mandala Center for Change. (n.d.). Theatre of the oppressed. http://www.mandalaforchange.com/site/applied-theatre/theatre-of-the-oppressed/

Mazzei, P., & Rashbaum, W. K. (2019, July 6). Jeffrey Epstein, financier long accused of molesting minors, is charged. *The New York Times*.

https://www.nytimes.com/2019/07/06/nyregion/jeffrey-epstein-arrested
-sex-trafficking.html

McGuire, D. L. (2010). *At the dark end of the street: Black women, rape, and resistance—a new history of the civil rights movement from Rosa Parks to the rise of black power.* New York: Vintage.

Meade, M. R. (2017). In the shadow of the coal breaker: Cultural extraction and participatory communication in the Anthracite Mining Region. *Cultural Studies, 31*(2–3), 376–399.

Mease, J. J., & Terry, D. P. (2012). [Organizational (performance] of race): The co-constitutive performance of race and school board in Durham, NC. *Text and Performance Quarterly, 32*(2), 121–140.

Moses, R., Kamii, M., Swap, S. M., & Howard, J. (1989). The algebra project: Organizing in the spirit of Ella. *Harvard Educational Review, 59*(4), 423–444.

Mouffe, C. (2000). *The democratic paradox.* London: Verso.

Mumby, D. K. (1997). The problem of hegemony: Rereading Gramsci for organizational communication studies. *Western Journal of Communication, 61*(4), 343–375.

NAACP. (n.d.). Nation's premier civil rights organization. https://www.naacp.org /nations-premier-civil-rights-organization/

Nayak, S. (2015). *Race, gender, and the activism of black feminist theory: Working with Audre Lorde.* New York: Routledge.

Northouse, P. G. (2016). *Leadership: Theory and practice* (7th ed.). Thousand Oaks, CA: Sage Publications.

Omolade, B. (1994). *The rising song of African American women.* New York: Routledge.

Orthy, N. (2016). Ella Baker, "address at the Hattiesburg Freedom Day rally" (21 January 1964). *Voices of Democracy: The U.S. Oratory Project, 11*, 25–43. http://voicesofdemocracy.umd.edu/ella-baker-address-at-the -hattiesburg-freedom-day-rally-21-january-1964/

Ospina, S., & Foldy, E. (2010). Building bridges from the margins: The work of leadership in social change organizations. *Leadership Quarterly, 21*(2), 292–307. https://doi.org/10.1016/j.leaqua.2010.01.008

Parker, P., Holland, D., Dennison, J., Smith, S. H., & Jackson, M. (2018). Decolonizing the academy: Lessons from the graduate certificate in partici-patory research at the University of North Carolina at Chapel Hill. *Qualitative Inquiry, 24*(7), 61–71.

Parker, P. S. (1996). Gender, culture, and leadership: Toward a culturally distinct model of African-American women executives' leadership strategies. *The Leadership Quarterly, 7*(2), 189–214.

Parker, P. S. (2001). African American women executives' leadership communi-cation within dominant-culture organizations: (Re) conceptualizing notions of nollaboration and instrumentality. *Management Communication Quarterly, 15*(1), 42–82.

Parker, P. S. (2003a). Learning leadership: Communication, resistance, and African American women's executive leadership development. *Electronic Journal of Communication, 13*(4/5), 46–59.

Parker, P. S. (2003b). Control, resistance, and empowerment in raced, gendered, and classed work contexts: The case of African American women. *Annals of the International Communication Association, 27*(1), 257–291.

Parker, P. S. (2004). *Race, gender, and leadership: Re-envisioning organizational leadership from the perspectives of African American women executives*. New York: Routledge.

Parker, P. S. (2005, March). *Race, gender, and leadership: (En)countering discourses that devalue African American women as leaders* [Paper presentation]. 27th Alabama Symposium, The Signs of Race Series on Literature, Race, and Ethnicity, Tuscaloosa, AL.

Parker, P. S. (2006, June). *Building capacity for leadership development and community activism among low-income African American teen girls and young women* [Paper presentation]. Moore Undergraduate Research Apprenticeship Program Seminar, Chapel Hill, NC.

Parker, P. S. (2019, December). *An afternoon with Ella Baker* [Keynote address]. Centro Cultural Larinda Santos Lobo, Santa Teresa, Rio de Janeiro, Brazil.

Parker, P. S., Oceguera, E., & Sánchez, J., Jr. (2011). Intersecting differences: Organizing [ourselves] for social justice research with people in vulnerable communities. In D. K. Mumby (Ed.), *Reframing difference in organizational communication studies: Research, pedagogy, practice* (pp. 219–242). Thousand Oaks, CA: Sage Publications.

Payne, C. (1989). Ella Baker and models of social change. *Signs, 14*(4), 885–899. https://doi.org/10.1086/494549

Payne, C. M. (2007). *I've got the light of freedom: The organizing tradition and the Mississippi freedom struggle*. Berkeley: University of California Press. (Original work published 1995)

Poletta, F. (2005). How participatory democracy became white: Culture and organizational choice. *Mobilization: An International Quarterly, 10*(2), 271–288.

Pratt-Clarke, M. (2013). A radical reconstruction of resistance strategies: Black girls and black women reclaiming our power using Transdisciplinary Applied Social Justice©, Ma'at, and rites of passage. *Journal of African American Studies, 17*(1), 99–114.

Puwar, N. (2004). *Space invaders: Race, gender and bodies out of place*. New York: Berg.

Rainie, L., Jurkowitz, M., Dimock, M., & Neidorf, S. (2012, March 15). *The viral Kony 2012 video*. Pew Research Center. https://www.pewresearch.org /internet/2012/03/15/the-viral-kony-2012-video/

Rankine, C. (2014). *Citizen: An American lyric*. Minneapolis, MN: Graywolf Press.

Ransby, B. (2001). Behind-the-scenes view of a behind-the-scenes organizer: The root of Ella Baker's political passions. In B. Collier-Thomas & V. P. Franklin (Eds.), *Sisters in the struggle: African American women in the civil rights–black power movement* (pp. 42–57). New York: New York University Press.

Ransby, B. (2003). *Ella Baker and the black freedom movement: A radical democratic vision*. Chapel Hill: University of North Carolina Press.

Ransby, B. (2017, October 21). Black Lives Matter is democracy in action. *The New York Times*. www.nytimes.com/2017/10/21/opinion/sunday/black-lives -matter-leadership.html?_r=0.

Ransby, B. (2018). *Making all black lives matter: Reimagining freedom in the twenty-first century* (Vol. 6). Oakland: University of California Press.

Rebecca A. (2018). My chair is made of plastic: Black women's seat at the feminist table—part 1. National Organization for Women. https://now.org/blog/my-chair-is-made-of-plastic-black-womens-seat-at-the -feminist-table-part-i/

Remnick, D. J. (2015, September 28). Blood at the root. *The New Yorker*, *91*(29), 26–34.

Rickford, R. (2016). Black Lives Matter: Toward a modern practice of mass struggle. *New Labor Forum*, *25*(1), 34–42.

Robnett, B. (1996). African-American women in the civil rights movement, 1954–1965: Gender, leadership, and micromobilization. *American Journal of Sociology*, *101*(6), 1661–1693.

Roeger, K. L., Blackwood, A. S., & Pettijohn, S. L. (2012). *The nonprofit almanac 2012*. Washington, DC: Urban Institute Press.

Rogers, C. R., & Farson, R. E. (1957). *Active listening*. Chicago: Industrial Relations Center of the University of Chicago.

Rogers, K. (2016, July 19). Leslie Jones, star of "Ghostbusters," becomes a target of online trolls. *The New York Times*. https://www.nytimes.com/2016/07/20 /movies/leslie-jones-star-of-ghostbusters-becomes-a-target-of-online-trolls .html

Santos, B. (2019). *Theatre of the oppressed, roots and wings: A theory of praxis*. Berlin: Kuringa.

Sapphire. (1996). *Push: A novel*. New York: Alfred A. Knopf.

Schillinger, H. (2017, November 16). We can't train our way to racial equity. Fakequity. https://fakequity.com/2017/11/16/we-cant-train-our-way-to -racial-equity/

Schwarz, R. M. (2013). *Smart leaders, smarter teams: How you and your team get unstuck to get results*. San Francisco: Jossey-Bass.

Scott, A. F. (1990). Most invisible of all: Black women's voluntary associations. *The Journal of Southern History, 56*(1), 3–22.

Scott, J. C. (1990). *Domination and the arts of resistance: Hidden transcripts*. New Haven, CT: Yale University Press.

Scott, K. D. (2016). Black feminist reflections on activism: Repurposing strength for self-care, sustainability, and survival. *Departures in Critical Qualitative Research, 5*(3), 126–132.

Sesko, A. K., & Biernat, M. (2010). Prototypes of race and gender: The invisibility of black women. *Journal of Experimental Social Psychology, 46*(2), 356–360.

Shaw University. (n.d.). *Shaw University brief history*. https://www.shawu.edu/About_Shaw/Historical_Perspective/?section=about-shaw

Shepherd, J., Wildt, M., & Salaberrios, D. (Producers), & Ivie, Brian (Director). (2019). *Emanuel* [Film]. Fathom Events.

Sigman, R. (1979). Service-learning: Three principles. *Synergist, 8*(1), 9–11.

Smith, L. T. (2005). On tricky ground: Researching the Native in the age of uncertainty. In N. K. Denzin & Y. S. Lincoln (Eds.), *The Sage handbook of qualitative research* (3rd ed., pp. 85–107). Thousand Oaks, CA: Sage Publications.

Smucker, J. M. (2014). Can prefigurative politics replace political strategy? *Berkeley Journal of Sociology, 58*, 74–82.

Spivak, G. C. (1988). Can the subaltern speak? In C. Nelson & L. Grossberg (Eds.), *Marxism and the interpretation of culture* (pp. 271–313). Urbana: University of Illinois Press.

Springer, K. (Ed.). (1999). *Still lifting, still climbing: African American women's contemporary activism*. New York: New York University Press.

Stack, C. B. (1975). *All our kin: Strategies for survival in a black community*. New York: Harper & Row.

Sudbury, J., & Okazawa-Rey, M. (2009). Introduction: Activist scholarship and the neoliberal university after 9/11. In J. Sudbury & M. Okazawa-Rey (Eds.), *Activist scholarship: Antiracism, feminism, and social change* (pp. 1–14). Boulder, CO: Paradigm.

Thomas, P. D. (2009). *The Gramscian moment: Philosophy, hegemony and Marxism*. Leiden, Netherlands: Brill.

Tonn, J. C. (2003). *Mary P. Follett: Creating democracy, transforming management*. New Haven, CT: Yale University Press.

Umoja, A., Stanford, K. L., & Young, J. A. (Eds.). (2018). *Black power encyclopedia: From "Black is beautiful" to urban uprisings* (Vols. 1–2). Santa Barbara: CA: Greenwood Press.

Velasquez, A., & LaRose, R. (2015). Youth collective activism through social media: The role of collective efficacy. *New Media & Society, 17*(6), 899–918.

Weick, K. E. (1995). *Sensemaking in organizations.* Thousand Oaks, CA: Sage Publications.

Weis, L., & Fine, M. (2013). A methodological response from the field to Douglas Foley: Critical bifocality and class cultural productions in anthropology and education. *Anthropology & Education Quarterly, 44*(3), 222–233.

Wells-Barnett, Ida B. (2012). *Southern horrors: Lynch law in all its phases.* Pittsburg, CA: Jeremiah B. Sanderson Leadership Institute. (Original work published 1892)

Wheatley, M. J. (1994). *Leadership and the new science: Learning about organization from an orderly universe.* San Francisco, CA: Berrett-Koehler Publishers.

White, E. F. (2010). *Dark continent of our bodies: Black feminism and the politics of respectability.* Philadelphia: Temple University Press.

Wilderson, F., III. (2003). Gramsci's black Marx: Whither the slave in civil society? *Social Identities, 9*(2), 225–240.

Williams, R. (2004). *The politics of public housing: Black women's struggles against urban inequality.* New York: Oxford University Press.

Young, I. M. (2001). Equality of whom? Social groups and judgments of injustice. *Journal of political philosophy, 9*(1), 1–18.

Yuval-Davis, N. (2012). Dialogical epistemology—an intersectional resistance to the "oppression Olympics". *Gender & Society, 26*(1), 46–54.

Index

Founded in 1893,
UNIVERSITY OF CALIFORNIA PRESS
publishes bold, progressive books and journals
on topics in the arts, humanities, social sciences,
and natural sciences—with a focus on social
justice issues—that inspire thought and action
among readers worldwide.

The UC PRESS FOUNDATION
raises funds to uphold the press's vital role
as an independent, nonprofit publisher, and
receives philanthropic support from a wide
range of individuals and institutions—and from
committed readers like you. To learn more, visit
ucpress.edu/supportus.

Made in the USA
Middletown, DE
11 January 2025